Preface

by George Eustice MP

My father never lived to see this book published but, true to character, he finished it all the same, shortly before passing away in October 2016 after a long battle with cancer.

The title, "To hell with the bank" was never in doubt and had been mooted for many years. On one hand it captures his sentiment towards Barclays Bank following our acrimonious legal dispute with them. On the other hand, it describes the journey that both we, and the bank's advisers, embarked on together during those tumultuous events of 1995. The lawyers and insolvency practitioners involved in the case apparently dubbed Barclays vs Eustice as "The Cornish Bloodbath", hence the sobriquet. Indeed, we were told that, in the aftermath, there had been a meeting of practitioners on both sides to discuss how to avoid such an unnecessary battle happening again.

Family, and the history of our family in the parish of Gwinear, mattered greatly to my father. Indeed it was what motivated him for most of his life. He felt a genuine duty as the custodian of the land our family had farmed - in some cases, for generations. Thus, it is no surprise that he describes the family and its history at some length in the book. He also considered the herds of pedigree South Devon Cattle and British Lop pigs to be part of the family.

My father was modest about his achievements in the book. He never warmed to people who bragged. Since he couldn't say it for himself then, and for the sake of completeness, let me use this foreword to say that Paul Eustice was a great innovator and pioneer. He was always coming up with new ideas. I remember as a boy returning home from school one day to find that my favourite toy tractor had been commandeered and a cardboard contraption built around it. My father, in the mid 70s, was an early instigator of in-field harvesting systems and had designed a rig that would enable winter cauliflowers to be simultaneously harvested and packed to create ergonomic efficiencies.

He then realised that the cost of wooden crates was a major factor affecting the profitability of the enterprise. So, he pioneered the use of polythene packaging, which was a fraction of the cost. Sceptics said that using polythene would not succeed because produce would overheat. However, they were wrong. In fact, the use of plastic packaging prevented dehydration and meant that his produce was always fresh and sold for a premium in the markets. Next, he designed new handling systems - using wooden bins to reduce the labour required to transport and manage produce in transit.

Some of his ideas might have been regarded as quirky but many of these became great successes. In 1979, after a very hard winter when a lot of crop was lost, he decided to plant strawberries and raspberries - he had always had a passion for fruit growing, which he mentions in the book. He then opened one of the first Pick Your Own fruit farms in Cornwall and, within a few short years, he and my mother had built it into a runaway commercial success. Every summer during the 1980s Trevaskis Farm would be inundated by people picking their own fruit. By the mid-eighties, he was growing no less than 30 different crops, either for Pick Your Own or sale in the Farm Shop. Today, it remains a tremendous success and a lasting legacy of his vision and foresight.

I remember being at college in the late 1980s studying farm business management. As one of the final projects, each student brought in the accounts for their own farm in order to analyse and measure performance against national benchmarks. The accounts for my father's business were off the clock in terms of sheer output per acre and in terms of gross profit due to multiple efficiencies and income streams derived from his many innovations. It confounded all business norms. However, there was a twist. Finance charges were also off the clock due to the highly geared nature of the business. This was almost unique at a time when bank base rates floated between ten and fifteen percent. The performance of the business was technically second to none but it needed to be.

Five years later, motivated by a desire to keep the oldest family farm within the fold - following the retirement of my great uncle - we put together an audacious project to expand the soft fruit business with a large enterprise of over fifty acres and an increase in the size of the winter vegetable business. The plan was sound but carried risks that were acknowledged in advance. All we needed was a bank that would show consistency and nerve. What could go wrong?

The final thing to say about my father is that he was a fighter, as Barclays Bank would learn to their great cost. In a loose-tongued moment, a group of consultants instructed by the bank let their guard down when doing some work on a farm in Kent. This farmer then delivered a tip-off that the bank was surreptitiously planning an ambush that would push our business into receivership. It seemed extraordinary and a complete breach of all the undertakings that had been given. Of course the business was highly geared as it always had been but there were still net assets of almost half a million pounds. The family had already put forward a radical plan to dispose of some assets that would have slashed debt by over a third and this had been praised by the bank's own agricultural adviser.

All my father had ever asked for was time and space. However, armed with the intelligence of an imminent attack, he assembled a high-powered team of lawyers, land agents and advisers to fight the bank should the worst happen. As well as top flight legal and accountancy firms, our team included David Neuberger QC who would later become Lord Justice Neuberger, the President of the Supreme Court.

When the bank launched its bungled attack, it got more than it bargained for. In the course of nine months there would be some 27 separate court orders or injunctions and the bank would spend more on legal and professional fees than it had lent the business in the first place as it set about trying to destroy one of its largest farming customers in the south-west.

There were a number of features that acted as an accelerant in Barclays vs Eustice. In particular, it became something of a proxy battle for two competing firms of west country solicitors - each vying for future business with Barclays. It was not in the interests of the solicitors advising the bank to seek an early end to the conflict. However, it would become a painful episode for all who were involved on both sides. In the aftermath, bank managers were moved away from Cornwall; regional directors were ushered towards voluntary exit deals; it provoked political tension at the top of leading accountancy and law firms; the bank was forced to swallow a bitter pill on its legal and professional fees and, most importantly of all, it resulted in a heavy blow to our family's farming business. There were no winners in the end.

For my part, at the age of just 22, I ended up having to step in to defend our family during a two week High Court trial as "litigant in person." Ranged against me were four or five trained lawyers employed by the bank at vast expense. However, we gave them a good run for their money. The entire episode was the most formative experience of my life. It sounds strange but after it was all over and a peace settlement was finally agreed, I found myself almost missing the conflict and acrimony in which I had been immersed. Peter Williams, our solicitor, had offered me the chance to join his team at Burges Salmon but I had a rather low opinion of the legal profession and the judiciary by that stage. Instead, I would end up on an inexorable path to politics taking a position at Business for Sterling to campaign against the euro. There is no shortage of acrimony to go round as far as debates about the EU are concerned.

Of the 27 court orders linked to our case, we won some and lost some. A high point was when the court intervened to partially turf the receivers out of the business in May 1995. In order to avoid imminent defeat in an application for there to be a court appointed receiver to replace the bank's chosen receiver, Andersons - who worked for the bank - were forced to surrender voluntarily and agree an order requiring them to step back and allow the family to take back control of day-to-day management.

However, there were low points too. One of the consequences of making peace with the bank was that we had to forego the opportunity to go to the House of Lords and overturn a somewhat bizarre judgement by the Court of Appeal related to legal privilege. This judgement was described as "extraordinary" by the trial Judge who heard our case in full and the Law Society had been open to funding an appeal to the

Lords since there were concerns from many senior legal experts about the impact the precedent could have on the integrity of the justice system.

You always have to accept the outcome of Court Judgements but you do not have to agree with them. Under the 1925 Law of Property Act, Parliament created a statutory right that allowed a landowner to create a tenancy on farmland regardless of what might be said in any mortgage deed. This was done for good reason. Land must be farmed in order to remain productive and the imperative of feeding the nation must be placed above the narrow commercial interests of moneylenders. Some of the Judgements relating to Barclays vs Eustice fettered that statutory law as originally conceived by Parliament. The Court of Appeal Judgement regarding legal privilege was tantamount to saying that exercising a simple right - enshrined in parliamentary statute since 1925 - was "iniquitous" and that legal due process should therefore be set aside. I consider that a rather ludicrous notion.

A few weeks after becoming an MP in 2010, I introduced a Private Members Bill, called the Secured Lending Reform Bill. It sought to rebalance the law away from the banks and their receivers in favour of enterprise and the entrepreneurs who are the backbone of our economy. It didn't make it through on the first attempt but this remains unfinished business and I hope that Parliament will one day reassert itself in this area of law. It would be a posthumous atonement for the events that my father was forced to endure.

George Eustice MP

Pistols at Dawn

'You can't beat a good dawn raid!' said Nick, as he sat in the living room drawing the final bit of life out of a café crème cigar.

'You take people by surprise and once you have possession of their assets then you've got all the cards and they have no options. It's over with quickly.'

Nick Kidd worked on the agriculture team at the accountancy firm, Grant Thornton, but he worked on many insolvency cases. Most of his work was for banks, but like everyone else on the high-powered team we had assembled, this time he was working for the other side. His task was to help defend our business against an onslaught from the terminators in the bank's debt recovery team. He was discussing the modus operandi of the banking and insolvency professions during part of our planning.

Seven months later, here we were, ready and prepared. Still, there was no getting away from the fact that this was something of a surprise. We had been fighting the bank for the best part of a year and things had come to a head two months earlier at a trial in the Bristol High Court. However, for the last month we had been in close negotiation with the bank and their solicitors about heads of terms for a settlement agreement. We thought everyone had had enough of fighting. Discussions had been good-natured. The outline of the deal was that the bank would keep two of the farms to sell and we would make payments to them in two tranches to secure possession of the remaining three farms and stock. The only remaining issue to be agreed was the precise timing of payments of the two tranches. We thought it was finally over but we would be forced to go to one final level of catharsis before the bank would finally capitulate.

The previous evening, I had been with my son, George, to meet the owners of a glasshouse nursery in Penryn and to discuss the terms of a rental agreement for the site as we started the task of putting our lives back together. On the way back, I had an anxious message from my wife. Two separate people from North Cornwall had called her to say that they had been approached by agents working for the bank. They had been asked to take part in a dawn raid to seize cattle in Gwinear the following morning. Our predicament was quite well known by this stage but the farming community knew whose side they were on.

It was a beautiful, still, Cornish morning but we had had no sleep the night before. Much work had been done through the darkness. We thought that "dawn raid" might have literally meant what it said but we waited and waited. Then we heard the aggressive sound of a convoy of lorries roaring down the road.

'Here we go.' I said.

'I will head out to meet them at the end of the lane' said my younger son, Giles.

'What will you tell them?'

Giles had a mischievous look on his face.

'Well, none of those articulated lorries will be able to turn around in the yard. So I might just invite them all to drive up the lane together. Then we can enjoy watching them reverse back out empty handed.'

How did we get here?

The lie of the land

Back in 1986 I was forty years old. Most people have changed course a few times in their twenties and thirties and forty is when they hope to find themselves on track. I was different. I'd been on the same track since boyhood: farming. I was doing what I always had done, and all I ever wanted to do, and living in the place I loved with the wife and children who are dearer to me than anyone else in the world. I was trying new techniques, improving our farm year by year, and paying my way.

In 1986, my wife Adele was 39, and beautiful and clever and healthy like our three children. We lived at Trevaskis Farm House, a generously built, two-storey granite place hundreds of years old, on the side of a hill, facing south over a gentle valley.

When I looked out of the front windows at Trevaskis, the fields beyond rolled up and over to Lanyon, Deveral, Gwinear (a hamlet), and Reawla (another hamlet). Two other Eustice family farms, an easy walk over the hills, were Bezurrel and Tregotha. From the west windows I could see Angarrack Hill Farm, which was ours too. The fields were odd shapes, irregular, grazed by cattle or growing crops in rotation, and divided by hedges or low drystone walls. The colours varied from deep green to emerald to gold and sage as the year rolled around, mostly under blue skies, because this was Cornwall, the long thin foot that England dips into the Atlantic. The weather is mild, although often cooled by sea breezes. Our part of Cornwall is near the furthest, narrowest part, where there is ocean all on three sides and choppy currents crashing onto the north coast.

St Ives Bay was three miles west of the house at Trevaskis, and Land's End, out of sight ahead, not much more than twenty miles south-west; Camborne, north-east behind us, was about three miles. Main line trains from Penzance to Camborne and Redruth, and ultimately London, ran quite close behind the house. The line cut across the part of our land nearest the road.

At forty, I worked every hour God sent, and when I wasn't working I was promoting my farm and my vegetables and livestock. It was all worth it; I was very happy.

We'd moved into Trevaskis Farm when we married in 1968. It belonged to my father, but it had been empty for a few years, and it felt as if it was waiting for us.

In 1965, when Dad bought the place, with its seventy acres – I'd have been nineteen then – I thought he was paying over the odds. We'd known for about a year that it would come on the market before Michaelmas because the farmer, Ben Casley, had let it be known he would soon sell up and retire. All news of interest within a twenty-mile radius was transmitted by the Cornish bush telegraph long before it appeared in the *West Briton*. Farmers gossiped in the lanes and over the hedges, in the pubs and at the markets. If your dog had fleas the news would be around the world and back before it had scratched.

Trevaskis was less than a mile north-east of our family farm at Tregotha so Dad was interested. The sale was going to be at the Red Lion Hotel in Camborne. I knew he wanted to bid, but it all depended. We were going there partly out of curiosity, as you do, to see how local prices were going. We were walking along Fore Street when he hesitated. 'You go on,' he said. 'I'll catch you up.'

'Where are you going?'

'I'm just popping over to see Mr Whitt and tell him what I'm thinking to do. Just to make sure it's all right.'

He headed off towards the National Provincial Bank, taking his tweed cap off as he crossed the road. He can't have been inside the bank much more than five minutes, and he caught up just as I got to the door of the Red Lion. The auction was in a smallish room, big enough for a dozen farmers under a drift of tobacco smoke. Some of them were just nosey. I knew they couldn't have paid for the farm gate at Trevaskis. A few, and we knew who they were, might be willing to bid quite hard.

Ronnie Coad was the auctioneer: a big fellow, authoritative, from nine miles south in Helston. He stood up and started the bidding, did his best - but got as far as £11,500 and stopped. He had to close the sale because Trevaskis Farm hadn't met its reserve.

My dad had a word with him afterwards and said he'd pay what Ben wanted, which was £12,000, so everybody was happy, except me. I thought it was too much. How wrong I was. A solid granite house, white-plastered, beautifully situated, with its own good-sized farm was a good deal even then.

And yet, I'd need a home of my own soon. At nineteen I was already sweet on Adele Olds, the daughter of a prosperous farmer twenty miles away in St Buryan on the Lizard; we'd met when I was sixteen. When my sister Catherine had married Adrian Clifton-Griffith the year before, my father bought Mount Pleasant farm with its 80 acres at Porthtowan, about twelve miles away, which they could work and rent from him and then later buy. Mary, the middle one of the three of us, had married John Tilly in the summer just past and they'd gone to live at Trewhella, which John rented.

As for me, he wanted me close by, not miles away; as the only son, and a born farmer, I would be useful. I would soon be responsible for the land and livestock at Tregotha, besides any farm I might have of my own. Granny Katy, he said, had once told him a man should never do any manual work after he was fifty. Dad reached that age in 1967, so he spent many of his working days in Camborne afterwards with Gwinear Farmers and other local companies where he was a director, or judging South Devon cattle at shows.

Trevaskis, therefore, being conveniently close to Tregotha, was where Adele and I would live. A couple of months before we married I was made a partner in G. Eustice & Son, along with my mother and father. That summer Adele and I used to go to Trevaskis Farmhouse at weekends to paint it and get it ready to live in. Cornish farms are built to last, if you look after them, and in our part – the low-lying spine of a narrow county - they stand on granite.

We came back from our honeymoon, settled, and had our children there, and my father and mother stayed at Tregotha where I'd been brought up. At some point, between the birth of Serena in '69, George in '71 and Giles in '74, I received Trevaskis Farm outright, by deed of gift from my father. As the years passed and the children grew, I became effectively the farmer of Tregotha, Trevaskis and Angarrack.

Tregotha Farm is where Catherine and Mary and I spent our childhoods. It is less than a mile south of Trevaskis on a granite ridge, down a lane from a minor road, with arable fields sloping away in all directions. It has always looked very much as Trevaskis did before we exposed its stonework; a wide frontage, two storeys, slate-roofed, plastered white, set on a hillside overlooking the fields. The outbuildings were set around a yard quite close to the house, and there was a big barn.

My grandfather George Henry Eustice bought Tregotha when Dad was six, in 1923. George Godolphin Osborne, the 10th Duke of Leeds, whose forefathers had been major local mine-owners, was selling. The decline of Cornish mining and, according to gossip, his own gambling habit, must have left him short of ready money.

George Henry Eustice was 38 when he bought Tregotha but he didn't live there; he and my Grandmother, Katy, stayed on at the neighbouring farm, Bezurrel, and had seven children in the end.

He probably had a farm worker's family living in Tregotha Farmhouse, I'm not sure. However, they must have left, because Dad moved in and rented it from Grandpa in 1939 when he married my mother, Inez Gwennap from Splattenridden.

There isn't a word that adequately sums up my childhood at Tregotha. People say 'idyllic' and you imagine endless summers. That goes nowhere near it. Nor does 'secure'. The deep roots that our family had in the parish of Gwinear and the surrounding area going back centuries gave me an enormous sense of pride in, and commitment to, our family and our farms.

I was the only son. Catherine was born in 1940; Mary in 1943 and I came along in January 1946. In those days, in Cornwall, it was pretty much taken for granted that daughters got married to men with other farms nearby and sons got married and carried on the family business. So while on no occasion did anyone loom over the four-year-old me, as I parked my pedal car overlooking the valley, and intone 'Some day, my son, this will all be yours' – the implication was there. I would be a farmer. *Here.* Like my father, his father, his father, and so on for as long as anyone could remember.

I learned to read and write and do sums at Miss Blight's in Camborne. I started there in 1951. Everybody knew Miss Blight's, a respectable, sturdy-looking Victorian house on a corner with a smart sign that announced Elmhurst Preparatory School. Catherine and Mary took me up the farm lane to the road every day, and we went in on the bus. We wore uniform of course. At five, boys were miniature men, in voluminous shorts to the knee, a shirt and school tie, a blazer with a badge, and a school cap. Long shorts always looked too big at first because your mother bought them that way, to last as long as possible. But we had to learn early to tie a necktie and our shoelaces too.

In retrospect, Elmhurst Preparatory School may have lacked a damp course. To this day I remember the musty smell of the back courtyard where we went at playtime. In summer we would walk in crocodile to Lowenac Gardens, just down the road, to play rounders and run races. We must have played sports there in the mild early weeks of the Autumn term as well because I still can't pass that park without smelling the smoke from burning leaves.

Sometimes my mother would drive into Camborne, collect me after school and take me shopping with her. She had to use coupons for some things. Sweets and sugar were still rationed in 1951 and meat didn't come 'off ration' until I was eight. She'd go into Edgar Harvey's butcher's shop and he'd cut off a little bit of hogs' pudding and stretch his burly arm over the counter with it balanced on the edge of a knife, so that I could take it. It was delicious. As was Olds Ice Cream; never bettered since.

I did what I was told, more or less, so I suppose Miss Blight did some good. At the time she seemed very strict. One day she stalked around the class picking up pencils from our desks and dipping them into some horrid-tasting liquid – Listerine? Castor oil? I have no idea what it was but she wanted us all to stop chewing pencil-ends, and the method proved effective.

It was a perfectly good small private school but I'm told I didn't appreciate my luck.

'You're a big boy now, Paul. D'you like school?' asked one of my sisters.

'I wish I'd never started it,' I said, gloomily.

I felt that way for a long time. I didn't dislike formal education but I was horrified to discover that I'd have to submit to it for years and years. So many more interesting learning experiences were to be had at Tregotha, where every season brought exciting new things to do. Harold Williams, who lived with his wife and nine children in the cottage adjoining our house, was like a second father to me. He was Dad's herdsman, looking after our prize-winning dairy cattle – South Devons, pure-bred and placid, chestnut brown with rose-pink noses and random patches of kinky curl on their coats. As a small boy I would join in with Harold and the farmhands doing what needed doing – planting, feeding or milking or whatever it was, according to the weather, the market, the time of day and the time of year. Harold had a corner of one of our fields to himself, where he and his wife grew extra vegetables and anemones and which he picked and sold to help support that big brood of children.

Harold took me to agricultural shows when my father couldn't go. I used to love that, climbing up into the lorry to sit with Harold, while he drove us off to Camborne or Penryn or the Royal Cornwall Show at Wadebridge. I would help him with our South Devons, giving them a wash and brush-up before they went into the ring. When Dad couldn't be there Harold would lead them in for showing and judging. I learned showing too; I kept chickens and Silkie bantams when I was at Miss Blight's. The star of my little brood was my White Wyandotte rooster. I got him into show condition and became a participant instead of just a helper. I was a happy boy when I won. I suppose it nurtured the spirit of competition and improvement, which was strong in all of us.

Tregotha was the kind of mixed farm you see less often these days and, for a boy, it was heaven. I probably knew the names of all our fields before I went to school. I can't remember a time when I didn't know them, and the fields at Bezurrel as well. At Tregotha we had Gassack, Inner Gassack, Higher Gassack, Hilly, Yard, Back Door, Orchard, Drannack, Tappard, Well, Mowey Field, Trenerth, Pump Meadow and several more. I could have woken up in any one of them and known where I was from the contour of the land and the nature of the hedge.

After the war my father had bought a six-wheel Austin ex-Army lorry, the kind that troops used to travel around in. If you were a small boy in the front passenger seat of a car in those days, you'd get stuck for miles behind these big lorries in the lanes, and you could wave at the squaddies inside and they'd grin and wave back. They'd be sitting on opposite benches down both sides under a big khaki tarpaulin stretched over a sturdy metal frame. When Dad bought his lorry, he took the frame off and made it into a flat-bed with deep wooden sides that folded down, so that he and the men could load it up with sugar beet – which fetched a good price then – and drive it over to Gwinear Road Station for transport to the sugar refinery.

The disused frame, he fixed to the ground. My sisters and I would clamber over it and swing upside down off it like a small troop of monkeys. We were never bored. I loved to play with water; there was a pond next to the lane at Tregotha and a vigorous stream at the bottom of the farm where my friends and I would spend hours building rafts out of barrels and trying to get them to float, or making water pistols out of reeds, to squirt at my sisters and each other.

Because my father had six siblings and my mother four, and they all lived within twenty miles of us, I had literally dozens of cousins and aunties and uncles to visit at holiday times. Not only aunts and uncles but also great-aunts and great-uncles. In the normal run of things, young people would marry and have children in their early twenties, so three generations or even four, all living within half a mile of each other, were common in every village. So even in the 1970s when Adele and I had our own young family, there were Eustices at Trevaskis - ourselves; at Tregotha – my parents; and at Bezurrel – my grandparents and Dad's much younger brother Derrick, with his wife and children.

Bezurrel, where Grandpa and Grandma lived, is north-east of Tregotha; a big place with a wide square yard surrounded by granite outbuildings – stables, haylofts, stores – next to an imposing double-fronted square house built of granite blocks, with quoins at the corners and around the windows. The house is quite grand and formal, even more so because it stands four or five feet above the farm lane to one side, facing south.

Grandpa lived to be 92. He would have been 21 at the start of the First World War and was farming with horses until the Second War at least. His early years of strenuous labour had toughened him. Change came slowly, a tractor here, a combine there, fewer horses – and although the old man was a hard taskmaster, Uncle Derrick and Aunty Dorothy were good-tempered and put up with him. My Uncle Derrick had grown up at Bezurrel and he had three daughters.

What Derrick and Grandpa loved to do, and Dad did without enthusiasm, was rear pigs. My father, from boyhood until he married and right through the war and Derrick's National Service, had done years of tough manual work at Bezurrel, where the British Lop pigs were famous, and I think he never wanted to see another slop bucket in his life. But the pigs came as part of the Bezurrel package, along with truculent old George Henry, so even-tempered Derrick was the one who took pigs to the shows and did well with them. His champion British Lops were fat, pale pink animals with backs dead straight, ear-flaps that flopped over their eyes, and tiny dainty trotters, like big ladies with tiny feet squashed into winklepickers.

My grandfather, George Henry Eustice, who outlived his wife Katy and died in 1977, had inherited Bezurrel from his own father John Edward, who had inherited it from the George Eustice who'd bought it – probably with money earned or inherited from mining – in 1863.

The records show Eustices getting baptised and married and buried at Gwinear Church from the early 1700s at least, when mining was what Cornwall was best known for. The mines yielded mainly tin, silver, cobalt and copper. There were local farmers and growers even then but mines were the real money-makers at Gwinear and Camborne. There's still a statue of local boy Richard Trevithick over at Camborne. In the early nineteenth century he invented an improved, high-pressure engine for pumping water out of the mines and carting the minerals by locomotive steam power. At that time Cornish mines inspired many local boys to become great engineers and work all over the world, just like Trevithick, but the mines steadily lost trade to foreign competitors. So the miners became farmers. Starting from 1863, my ancestors were farming Bezurrel, but the gentle hills and higgledy-piggledy fields around here are still dotted with disused shafts and tips, a constant reminder of a lost industry.

Angarrack Hill Farm had been bought by my father in 1958 and eight years later he added Burnthouse Farm to it. Because there wasn't a farmhouse at that one (the name's a clue) we farmed the two as one piece.

The long low granite cottage at Angarrack was always occupied, when I was a child, by Kenny Hollow who worked for us. The most underrated job in the world is probably farmhand. As I grew up, I learned an enormous amount from people like Kenny Hollow and Clare Treloar (Clare, a man's name) and Harold Williams. Most of the pickers and farm labourers lived in nearby hamlets and their families, like ours, had been farming for generations. They knew a lot.

A townsman might glance out of a train window as he tears past on his way from Penzance to London, and see without interest a man letting cows into a field or towing some unidentifiable machine behind a tractor. If the image registers at all, he would imagine it was mindless work. But if they changed places, the townsman wouldn't know if a cow was sick or what the machine was for; he couldn't look at a field and know if the crop was wheat or barley. The farmhand can. He can spot a cow that's off colour and knows, not just when and how to operate the tractor and the seed drill, but why he's planting corn into that field and not the one next door, and what pests and diseases are likely to threaten it as it grows. That kind of understanding is taken for granted, and therefore it's value is underestimated. You don't know how much you know, because everyone around you knows it too.

I learned new things just about every day, from my father and his workers as I grew up; but it all felt like fun.

Family ties

In 1939 at the start of the Second World War my father George Eustice, just married, rented Tregotha from his father George Henry Eustice, who stayed at Bezurrel. Farming was a protected occupation during the war, so Dad was not called up, but I'm not sure about his brothers. I know most farms had a big labour shortage and the Government ordered them to produce whatever the nation demanded or pay the penalty. Derrick, my father's youngest brother at Bezurrel, could legally leave school at 14 in those days, but even so he would be much too young to run the whole farm; and after the war every boy was called up at 18 anyway to do National Service for two years. So what with one thing and another George, as the eldest son, farmed Tregotha but did a hell of a lot of work for his father at Bezurrel as well.

I grew up proud of him. He was a figure of consequence locally. I think he had learned, as a boy, the same confidence I had. If you're part of a family with a long heritage and a solid reputation, that happens. People respected my Dad and when I went out with him I unconsciously knew he had a good name wherever we went.

He was a farmer through and through, and his business interests reflected that. As a director of West Cornwall Meat Traders he would go to all the local livestock markets to see and buy, and when he could, he took me. We were at Helston Market once when he'd just bought me a new pair of hobnailed boots. I was about six then, and I loved wearing hobnailed boots, and I swaggered out of the shop, quite the lad, with my new pair tied together by their long laces and slung over my shoulder. At the market, a shrimp amid the hubbub of shouting men and lowing cattle, I stood behind the auctioneer with Dad. My right hand held the bootlaces and a finger was enough to swing those heavy boots satisfyingly back and forth, back and forth, like a pendulum, while my father, beside me and above my head, bid on some calves. What I didn't know was that the boots were banging the auctioneer on the backs of his legs and when he turned around, he wasn't too pleased to find that he'd sold me some calves as well.

Cattle were Dad's thing, and his interest took him into public life. He was involved with South Devon Herd Book Society and the National Farmers Union, so I grew up hearing these names and knowing how important our herd was.

Father also took me to the slaughterhouse at Camborne, where I stood idly by while he talked business with the manager there. He also took me to Tonkins Bakers, where Dad was a director. They used to keep pigs at Roskear, on the outskirts of town, on all the waste bread and cakes from their shops and restaurant, and Dad was responsible for buying those pigs and making sure they were looked after properly.

When I was seven or eight, on cold winter weekends he began taking me to shoot woodcock with him in the valleys below the farm. I wasn't particularly keen on shooting, but I was glad to be there, learning about it, along with him and his dogs.

We still had horses when I was young. In 1948, when a valuation was done, there were six. Dad kept the horses for a long time because there were some jobs they were better at.

I have a copy of that valuation. I don't know why it was compiled, but it is dated 5th April, a significant date in the tax year. It itemises deadstock - that's anything lifeless such as tools and machinery – crops still in the ground, or stored as seed, or ready for consumption, or animal feed; and livestock. It is many pages long and evidence that ours was a well-equipped, well-managed farm. The deadstock alone was worth about £1,500, which at the time was big money. Easily enough to buy you two three-bed semis in a town.

My father was always looking to improve Tregotha. When I was a boy he had a two-seater David Brown Cropmaster that was ideal for me because when I came home from school, I'd run out and get on that tractor with whoever was driving it and sit and watch what they were doing. I quickly learned to drive it, and sometimes I'd steer while Harold Williams sat behind me working the binder.

Tregotha in 1948 had everything a mixed farm could need, from rollers, drills and a cultivator to sterilising equipment for the dairy, houses for the hens and – that April – half an acre of uncut broccoli worth £25, four acres of spring cabbage valued at £200; broccoli boxes, mats, chitting trays (for sprouting), rabbit netting, binder twine, small tools etc. £600; broccoli seed, £72.10s, and 50,000 anemone corms, to a value of £60. Immediately after the war, farmers were valued and asked to do more as the country tried to produce the food that it needed and to end years of ration books. Farming was profitable.

-

Mother came from Splattenridden Farm, but she didn't really. She had been born at Deveral, which is much closer to Tregotha. Her father, my grandfather, was Robert Gwennap from Ludgvan, down by the Lizard. He was one of nine children of a market gardener. You'd think there could be no possible harm that came from such beginnings but, to this day, more than 130 years since his birth, there are still people in the family who don't want to repeat what they were told about Robert Gwennap and I never have managed to find out where he's buried.

I've pieced together what I can. Robert had a couple of elder brothers who worked in the copper mines around the Lizard. I believe he stayed at home, helping his father, until around the end of the Second Boer War in 1902; then he sailed to South Africa, where he got a job in the gold-mines. Ten years later he came back with plenty of money and the 1911 census shows Robert Gwennap farming Deveral (less than half a mile from Tregotha) with his sister Louisa. Within a month or two of that census, Louisa married a man from Ludgvan and went back there. Robert, brought his own bride, Norah Jane Richards – also from Ludgvan – to live with him at Deveral. My Granny Katy knew her when they were both young wives. She told me Norah was a lovely person and they were great friends.

In the next few years the Gwennaps had two daughters. The third, my mother Inez, was born in 1917. I don't know what the problem was at Deveral, probably just the usual farming ups and downs unsupported by a sufficiently large reserve of capital, but the Gwennap family had to move out when my mother was less than a year old. They got Downs Farm instead – steep, windy land near the cliffs, on the coast north-west of Camborne. Years later, mother's older sisters told her how on moving day they put her in her Moses basket onto the farm cart with all their goods and chattels, and walked the four or five miles alongside their mother while their father led the horse. It makes a sad and bitter picture.

Norah Jane's father Charles owned Downs Farm so they would be safe there whatever happened. Two more babies came along, both girls, but at Easter 1923 when Norah Jane was pregnant again, she fell ill. She died in Camborne and Redruth Hospital. There would be no sixth child.

Two days later her father Charles Richards, a widower, died. Norah Jane's only brother was Charles Paul Richards - known as Paul; married, but childless. The story goes that 'he'd hardly got time to pull his boots on before he was over at Downs Farm looking to interfere.' That was how it seemed anyway. Paul

Richards may have been tactless, or maybe Robert was one of those people who won't listen to advice however well meant. But relations between the two men, now that Paul was Robert's landlord, did not improve. I suspect it was Paul's fault. I've wondered why there was a problem and asked some very old people whether Robert was idle, or a lazy farmer, but he seems to have been thrifty and hard-working. They told me how he would lead his horse and cart along the clifftop, stop, rope himself to the cart and slide down the hundred-foot cliff to the shore. Wrecking, we called it; picking up driftwood, or whatever was going. He'd tie the wood into a bundle, lash it to the hanging rope, and clamber back up hand over hand. At the clifftop, he'd give his horse a smack, and the two of them, horse and man, would haul the roped-up bundle up and onto the cliff and get it home to use as fencing or firewood or whatever he needed. I suppose a climb on the cliffs of North Cornwall would be child's play to a man who'd worked in the deepest gold mines in the world.

Robert Gwennap either found a housekeeper to look after his five little girls, or a succession of housekeepers, I don't know. As he carried on farming at Downs the animosity between him and his brother-in-law did not diminish and after three years of being told how to run his business and bring up his children, he could take no more. Robert strode over to Splattenridden, confronted Paul Richards and his wife, and told them if they were so clever, they could damn' well look after Downs Farm and the girls as well. He'd had enough and was going away to make some money for his family. He put the girls, aged from 15 down to about four, on the train from Camborne to Hayle and Uncle Paul Richards collected them from the station.

The younger ones were sent to school but they were all working on Splattenridden Farm every spare moment before they reached 14, which was school-leaving age then. Much later, Uncle Paul and Aunty Mott had their only child, a son, called Charlie.

All the girls married Cornish farmers and had settled lives. What I can't figure out is whether any of them ever saw their father again after 1926. Jane, the oldest, was 14 when Robert put them on the train at Camborne Station, and 16 when he came back. He definitely went to South Africa but I have found no record of how he got there. My mother had a photograph of him, taken sometime in those two years in South Africa. A somewhat` down-at-heel man stands and stares at the camera in a city street, very likely in Johannesburg.

He did not return alone. Mr Robert and Mrs Evelyn Gwennap embarked together in Cape Town on the P&O ship *Berrima,* and arrived in London on 12th October 1928. Evelyn gave her age as 30 and Robert said he was 42 (he was 44). He gave his occupation as 'gold miner'. The last country where they had been resident was South Africa and their English address would be in Marazion, Cornwall.

We are not sure who Evelyn was. But this time, in leaving South Africa, Robert had given up on a country, and an industry, that had changed considerably in the fifteen years since he first left it. The big gold mining companies could make a profit only by digging deeper and employing cheap labour. There was political and inter-racial conflict. It was a troubled place.

Anyway, they came back, and whether or not they intended to stay who knows? There is no further information for six years. So far as I know he may never again have even visited Cornwall, because, one Saturday afternoon in June 1934, Robert Gwennap, aged 50, riding a bicycle out of Aylesbury Street, Pimlico, London, onto the Thames Embankment at Grosvenor Road, was killed by a GPO van.

There is a newspaper report of the accident, which gives his address at 25 Aylesbury Street; there is a death certificate; but there is no record of his job or his wife. There is no will and no record of a burial. All we have is a letter from the Westminster Coroner to Aunty Evelyn Gwennap (not the new wife) referring, sympathetically and delicately, to matters that she has mentioned in previous correspondence. What those matters were, I've yet to discover.

-

My mother was loving, strict, but competent and ambitious, like my father. They were a good match. Their backgrounds were very different. Coming from Ludgvan, quite a hotbed of Methodism, her father Robert may have been brought up a Methodist; I'm not sure. His brother, her Uncle Howard Gwennap, and his wife (another, older Evelyn) were very strict, in that line. Anyhow her relations on Norah Richards' side were all Church of England, like us, and Mother seems to have been perfectly happy to marry into our family.

We all went to Gwinear Church on Sundays and as children we attended Sunday School. For local families the Church was socially indispensable. After the service people would gather in clusters in the churchyard, chattering like birds. It was one of the places (like village pubs, post offices, and town markets) where families from outlying farms could meet their neighbours. Until the late 1950s working people rarely had a phone at home. Significant farmers did, if they could pay for a line onto their land, and they drove family cars too, but nearly everybody else had to put pennies in the village coin-box telephone and walk or use a bicycle or a bus. If a new family came to live in the village – which didn't happen often – they could expect a visit from the Vicar and an invitation to join the congregation.

My mother had entirely settled in at Tregotha and we were all young and fast asleep, late one summer's evening, when our parents and Uncle Tom and Aunty Jane, Mother's oldest sister, were sitting at the kitchen table talking and drinking glasses of sherry from a decanter – and somebody knocked at the back door.

'Who's that?'

'I'll go and see.'

The others listened. They heard my father – 'Howard! ... Evelyn - Good to see you...'

'Quick!' hissed my mother, jumping to her feet. In a flash, she'd gathered up the glasses and shut them in a cupboard.

'Hallo, how are you!' I imagine her coming forward, flushed and affectionate. She did feel warm towards them but none of Robert Gwennap's girls had ever turned into Methodists.

Uncle Howard and Aunty Evelyn had walked over to Tregotha, they said, because it was such a lovely evening. All six of them sat and talked and virtuously drank cups of tea. Darkness fell, the gaslight was lit and conversation faltered. The human eye is drawn to movement. And they were all staring at the decanter, still half full and in the middle of the table.

'My,' said Tom, 'how they flies do go for that vinegar.'

-

Rituals were the cogs that kept the years rolling around. On Bonfire Night we'd have a massive fire and fireworks with the Pascoe family (who had a house on the Tregotha Farm lane) and Harold Williams and his wife; at least fourteen children and half a dozen adults, often more, and a straw-stuffed Guy on top of the bonfire. You could buy fireworks at any age then, and they were always in the newsagents' shops at Camborne from October until November 5th. Bangers were a big favourite, and the small wiggly brown ones we all called Jumping Jacks, and Catherine Wheels that you had to nail to a tree, and rockets called things like Lightning Flash or Massive Fire; if you were lucky you got a box of your own, and compared fireworks with your friends before the big night. Even now, the smell of them brings back a glorious sense of anticipation. My father always set fireworks off after the Bonfire was lit, and we all waved sparklers about. Nobody ever had fireworks at any other time of year.

We usually spent Christmas Eve with the Caseys at Marazion - not relations but good friends of my father since Mr Casey engraved all the cups my father won. At Christmas and Easter we reinforced the family bonds. On Christmas Day we would have Christmas Dinner with Uncle Paul, Aunty Mott, and all my mother's sisters and their families at Splattenridden. On Boxing Day we did the same thing all over again at Bezurrel with Uncle Derrick, Aunty Dorothy and our grandparents.

In those days Camborne had greengrocers and butchers, fishmongers and bakers. Everyone expected seasonal food. The greengrocers stocked cabbages and potatoes and onions in winter, and lettuce and tomatoes and cucumbers only in summer. Roast chicken was a treat. At Christmas, and only at Christmas, tangerines and dates came into the shops. In June there were strawberries and new potatoes and peas. In September, blackberries. If you had an orchard - and there was a lovely one at Bezurrel – then in the autumn, surplus apples were set out, carefully separated, in neat lines on newspaper, in the loft, to keep cool. A glut of soft fruit was made into preserves or put into pies because most people didn't have a fridge. Butchers sold game in season and made their own sausages and pies. Fish was locally caught.

It's easy to be nostalgic about all this, although today we have year-round fruit and vegetables in varieties undreamed-of in the early 1950s and it all makes life more interesting. Women don't trail about with shopping bags the way they used to and, in the cities; it is common for everything to arrive at the door in a supermarket van because whole households are busy working to pay the rent or the mortgage. On the whole, most people are better off. We were probably dirtier, and diseases like measles were common, but we were much fitter. In the fifties, you very rarely saw a fat child.

In summer, my mother and father often took us to Newquay Boating Lake. Mary seemed to get wet, or fall in, just about every time we went, to shrieks of laughter from Catherine and I. With the seaside, and loads of cousins, on three sides of our farm, we spent a great deal of time at different beaches. There's a photo of me, aged about one, on Hayle Towans - only three miles from Tregotha - where one of Dad's aunties had a beach hut. We'd stay all day sometimes, or we'd go to Praa Sands or Kelynack Sands with cousins from Trewennack. My mother and her sisters were all close and our cousins remain so even now. We played cricket on the beach in summer and board games in each other's houses in winter. Very few people had television then but everybody knew how to play snap and snakes and ladders and do jigsaws by the time they were about five.

The first time I saw TV was on Coronation Day, early in June 1953. I'd have been seven and a half. Schoolchildren got flags and coronation mugs and all sorts of free merchandise for the Coronation, and many people splashed out on a TV set and invited friends and relations to celebrate on the big day. My father's uncle was one of those. He lived in a big house, Tolroy Manor, that had mains electricity (which we didn't, yet) and was within reach of a transmitter – so he'd bought a television. We gazed in wonder at the live broadcast of the coach and horses, the crowds, and the Abbey, with the unsmiling young woman in her top-heavy crown. These tiny, blurry, and black-and-white images from faraway Westminster Abbey were the future.

Getting ready to farm

Coronation Year, 1953, was when life began to get slightly more comfortable. My mother and father hired a builder, William Trevarthen from the village of Wall, to build an extension onto the north side of Tregotha, with a big kitchen at ground level and a bedroom above.

I wish I could remember whether we got electricity that year or the next. We'd had a generator on the farm for as long as I could remember, but it was kept in an outbuilding, and if we all came home in the dark Dad used to head over to start it up. As he set off he'd warn us kids that we'd got five minutes to get into bed. If we weren't tucked up and quiet when he came in, he'd switch the current off again and we'd be plunged into darkness. I do know that Tregotha was finally connected to the grid one Christmas. A fellow from the Electricity Board arrived to do the work and, because it was Christmas Eve and we were all lively and excited by our new bright lights, my father managed to get him very jolly indeed.

At the start of the autumn term my parents and Miss Blight decided that I should take the entrance exam for Truro Cathedral School. I hadn't applied myself to lessons with outstanding enthusiasm until that point, but I was now nudged forward with no choice in the matter. All that winter Miss Clifton, who was one of our teachers at Miss Blight's, gave me extra lessons at her home in Roskear, and the following year I took the exam and passed.

In September of 1954, aged eight and three quarters, the plan was that I would become a weekly boarder in an old and prestigious school twenty-one miles from home.

Truro Cathedral School had been educating boys like me since the Middle Ages, so there wasn't much I could do to surprise them. It had been promoted from a chantry school to a Grammar School in 1549, but when (in the 1870s) Truro got grand enough to boast its own Cathedral, the Church of England identified it as a suitable forcing-house for choristers and renamed it.

You could get a choral scholarship if you sang sweetly. I wasn't going to qualify. I ventured a couple of notes - quite melodious, I thought – and the choirmaster muttered something rude about a foghorn.

When I started there wasn't a dormitory place, so I had to be a day boy. Truro Cathedral School had developed piecemeal in different parts of town, so pupils were based in this or that building according to age and were constantly trotting, or idling, around the streets to get to a classroom here, a laboratory there. It kept us fit, and was certainly good for me. At nine, I showed promise as a runner, and I went on to excel at rugby.

By today's standards the school was small: two or three hundred pupils. Mr Mischler, the headmaster, had already been Head for seventeen years when I turned up in 1954. I started at Copeland Court, where there was a separate Head called Mr Gibson and the pupils were as young as seven. Later I graduated to the prep school at Trevaunance and at thirteen to the Senior School at Cathedral Close; by then I'd been taught in just about every corner of Truro at some point. We attended Kenwyn Church as juniors and the Cathedral, later, for morning assembly – which must never be missed. And of course we had sports fields.

Scuttling through the streets in a downpour with a satchel full of books was enough to make you long to skip into a cinema or a tea-room or even, if you'd dared, an early train home. I never did become a boarder. By the time a dormitory place became available, I'd come to enjoy the commute with school friends from Camborne, and wanted to be on the farm every hour I could. So I remained a day-boy – six days a week, because there were classes on Saturday mornings as well.

My mother got me onto the fast train every day by driving like a dervish the three miles to Camborne Station. Quite often she'd grab the car keys and leave with me at ten to eight. I had to catch the 08.04am from Camborne or I wouldn't reach school in time for Assembly. She never failed. Off we hurtled and fortunately, there was never a broken-down tractor in the lane or a milk float holding up traffic. There wasn't much traffic at all, then.

I was sporty; the school magazine shows that I won races and came close to top in athletics as well, but I never came first in anything academic. I was pragmatic and I didn't see much point in excelling at history or English Literature, never mind Latin. I didn't mind learning them but I wasn't going to need them. I did my homework; I got by in everything, but was always certain that I would be a farmer. I would need some maths, biology, geography - I liked geography a lot - and good written English. What I really needed to understand was stock breeding and agriculture, buying and selling, and I would learn about those things at home.

I'd stay late at school to practice cricket or running or rugby, but in good weather, when the bell rang at ten to four I'd be off like a hare to catch the Cornish Riviera Express from Paddington. In those days it stopped at Gwinear Road Station and I could be home by twenty past four, and out of school uniform and working on the farm within ten minutes. I did my homework later. It would have been a crime to waste daylight hours indoors.

Harold Williams used to take me ferreting, and that was how I came to have a ferret of my own, called Freddie. My friend Christopher from Henver Farm used to come with me at weekends sometimes. You needed two people - one to watch the ferret and one to dive on the rabbit as soon as it came out of the warren and into a net. Rabbits love green leafy vegetables and Father grew a lot of them. Christopher would stand on one side of the hedge, I'd be on the other, and Freddie would dive down into the warren and do the job he was born for - chasing a rabbit until it came up into fresh air and the net. Harold taught me to kill rabbits quickly and humanely and Freddie and I did a good job.

When I started at Truro Cathedral School I got the best present ever from my father; a donkey called Prince. My Uncle, Johnny Benney, had found Prince for me and I was almost too excited to speak. He could pull a shay – a kind of little bucket seat made out of old planks, supported between two heavy old bicycle wheels. I learned to harness him and in summer I'd walk him down to village fetes, at Gwinear Church or Rosewarne Manor, to raise money for Church funds by offering rides to little children. Later on at harvest time my father got me a cart for him and Prince and I would help the men by carting sheaves of corn.

I was always a schoolboy on sufferance. For me, real life began when I got back to Tregotha. In the holidays, I had cousins and friends of more or less my own age to visit. We fished, we messed about with engines, we rode bikes, and although we had a lot of fun - and nearly all of them were from farming families - I was notoriously happiest at home, with Prince and Freddie and the sheep and cows and pigs and all the other work that needed doing on the farm. My parents didn't go away on holiday but they did get a few days' respite quite often by going to shows elsewhere in the south-west.

When we were 13, Truro Cathedral School expected us to join the Combined Cadet Force and do drill or go away, occasionally, on exercises. The alternative was a scowl from Mr Mischler

whenever he saw you. So I joined - and it was good for me. I was no Idle Jack to start with but the Cadets instilled meticulous attention to detail and, above all, unquestioning obedience - which will probably come in useful if ever I need rescuing by helicopter. At the time I disliked polishing my boots and wearing the uniform. The coarse khaki worsted prickled like sacking. Wriggling as I stood to attention and unable to have a surreptitious scratch, I longed for promotion to NCO and a decent shirt.
-

I meant to leave school in July 1962 after my O levels. This would have been perfectly possible because I worked hard and passed six of the seven subjects I took. However, my wily schoolmaster persuaded me that I really should stay on a term to re-take French. It would be useful, he said. It was a white lie. I knew, and he knew I knew, that he really wanted me on the rugby team. I'd been on the Senior School's team when I was only 15, and we'd had a great season, playing against Plymouth College, St Boniface, Camborne School of Mines, Redruth Grammar and other good amateur teams. I'd also been the County Champion 400-yard runner and this summer, in a term full of O levels and cricket, I'd run for Cornwall in the All England Championships at Hull.

So I didn't mind staying on for the autumn term because I made many friends through the sports I was good at; and I did pass French. However I'd already begun to develop a life away from school. I played for both Camborne Colts and Camborne Rugby Club and I'd made friends at Praze Young Farmers. I couldn't drive because I was still only 16 but my friend Alan Cock had a car and we used to go around together. My sisters gave me lifts too.

I left school for good at the Christmas of 1962, and anyone who lived through that winter will remember it. It was the coldest since 1947. That last week before Christmas, I had no idea what was about to happen. I'd left school, we had a new lorry to pull our vegetables to the market and I was keen to get on with the job. Also, I could look forward to passing my driving test because I'd be 17 in January.

Maybe snow began falling on Christmas Eve; I am not sure. But in my mind's eye I can still see big snow crystals drifting down and settling, one still, icy afternoon, and blanketing the fields. It settled, and stopped; the weather was too bitter, somebody said, for more snow. That year Mother was making Christmas dinner for all her sisters and their families, but on the day we didn't have any water because all the pipes were frozen. I had to struggle up to Reawla village to fetch water in churns so Mother could get on with the cooking.

On Boxing Day there was a blizzard. By New Year the roads were totally blocked, and we couldn't get up the lane for the drifts, many feet deep. According to the TV, foolish travellers were having to be dug out of cars and birds and beasts were dying all over the country. Hardly any British houses had central heating, fuel was scarce and expensive, and older people died of hypothermia.

It was a disastrous season for us. Come March, when the thaw began, we had just two acres of cauliflower left out of thirty we'd planted. The few that survived were a variety called Seal Hayne 48. They'd been planted from seed by a friend of my father's from Gwithian called Charlie James. He was expert at seed breeding and he'd spread this trial crop with the help of students from Seal Agricultural College. I knew his son Geoffrey – my father had run a day's instruction in livestock husbandry for the Young Farmers, and he'd come over to Tregotha for that. We became firm friends, and still are. But that winter taught me a lesson. Weather can never be forecast as far ahead as a farmer needs.

Mary and Catherine were home, and busy around the house, and we all had extra work keeping the livestock well fed and watered, but we were getting stir crazy, I think, after the first six weeks of it. Father had to lay off our lorry driver because we had nothing to sell. There seemed no end to that winter.

I had to give up running. I'd promised my schoolmaster that I'd keep on competing but there was no chance to train around Tregotha that winter. Anyway, while nowadays there are enthusiasts training along every clifftop path and bridleway, in those days running alone in the countryside was downright eccentric. My nearest cinder track was at Par, a 27 mile journey, and the only proper running track was 65 miles away at Plymouth. My energy would go into rugby instead; although that winter, there were no games until almost the end of the season.

I passed my driving test in March. The lanes were puddled with black water and grubby snow was heaped on the verges. I hadn't had to attend a driving school; Clare Treloar had taught me, first on tractors, and then around the farm and down at Penzance, where there was a circuit. Driving gave me independence. I could seize all the opportunities that the Young Farmers offered – especially proficiency tests in livestock and ploughing and growing. I remember going to a ploughing test a few miles from home at Townsend. Austin Delbridge was instructing us and he said

'Who are you then?

'Paul Eustice from Tregotha,'

'Well my good boy,' he said 'I should think you'd have enough ploughing to do at home, never mind coming up 'ere.'

'Yes, but I want to know how to do it properly. I want to be taught by an expert.'

It's a principle worth applying to most things. The Young Farmers ran competitions and encouraged me to learn public speaking, which has been amazingly useful. I learned from Willy Pascoe, who'd taught my father before me. I'd never have got that skill anywhere else. Later in life, in roles such as Committee Chairman, Guest Speaker on organic gardening, and Defendant in Court, it enabled me to speak confidently in public.

In April of 1963 I persuaded my father to buy a second seed drill, because Clare Treloar was doing all the cauliflower drilling and with me drilling as well, the job would go faster. Also, I was analysing the lessons learned that winter. I was in two minds about cauliflower. It had been almost a dead loss when the ground froze under snow, and I wanted to plant something else next year. I thought of asparagus and different things and finally settled on celery. We knew Brooks Brothers, the vegetable wholesalers from Wolverhampton Market, and Dad's contact there took us up to Lincolnshire to show us how celery was grown. This year we were too late, but in '64 I did plant some, with my drill, and when the winter of 64-65 proved to be another harsh one we'd got ours pulled, and off to market, when the farmers up in the Midlands and North couldn't harvest theirs at all. I taught Mrs Mitchell and Mrs James and Mrs Hampton from Reawla to pull celery and I carried quite a lot to sell to the shops around Cornwall. We even supplied the Campbell's Soup factory that icy winter.

It must have been beginner's luck, because I never got such an outstanding celery crop again. Fortunately most winters we also grew about 30 acres of cauliflowers and 12 acres of spring greens, enough to load and keep a lorry running through the winter months. We'd plant 25 to 30 acres of spring barley and maybe some dredge corn (oats and barley mixed, for feed) and some mangles and hay, for the cattle. I was always interested in new ways of looking after and feeding the animals, especially the South Devons. None of us knew about silage making yet.

Harold Williams became increasingly weak. The poor fellow was diagnosed with multiple sclerosis in 1964, so my sisters and I looked after the South Devons from then on, and I think it comforted Harold to know we were doing a good job. He still lived in a house on our land. He'd taught me about showing as well as animal husbandry and, thanks to him, I was able to take a steer to the Smithfield Show that year.

Kenny Hollow was more active with the pigs. In the freezing winter of early '63 we'd converted a building at Connor Downs, about a mile away, as a piggery, and Kenny Hollow would go over to them from Angarrack Farm. Dad kept only commercial pigs. He would take eight or ten Lop gilts from Derrick at Bezurrel, and we'd get a large white boar to cross on them. I went with my father to a breeder at St Agnes to find one that would be suitable. I remember carrying their food over to Connor Downs in the evenings after a day's work; we used to mill and mix our own corn and concentrate at Tregotha.

In the late sixties and early seventies, the older generation began to consult Kelsall Steele, the family accountants, and our solicitors Trott and Battell. Uncle Derrick farmed Bezurrel, my father farmed Tregotha, and one day, far, far in the future (as it seems when you're eighteen) I could expect to inherit Tregotha myself. So in the next ten or fifteen years a number of routine moves would be made; a partnership, inter-family gifts of strictly limited value, a couple of leases – all designed to minimise tax on the deaths of farming Eustices, while making sure that the land remained in the family. At the back of my mind I was preparing, not just for life as a farmer, but life as custodian of the land. Bezurrel and Tregotha, side by side, were the Eustice family's heritage.

That's what made learning worth while. I became competent to care for my father's fifty head of South Devons, ten to fifteen breeding sows, and about 120 acres of good well-kept farmland. I gained confidence and was soon joined by Michael Thackerer. He'd been in the year below mine as a schoolboy at Truro, and his father was herdsman for my grandfather at Bezurrel. Michael wanted to come and work at Tregotha with Clare Treloar largely because he could learn more. Grandfather, in his day, had been an early-adopter of tractors when many other farmers still relied on horsepower. Innovation has a downside, which is that you're stuck with the latest, best technology of 1927 when everyone else is using shiny new improvements on the original. At Bezurrel they got by with single-seater tractors so crotchety that Michael wasn't allowed to use them. We had modern two-seaters that worked. So Michael sat on the tractor working with Clare Treloar while I went off to shows with my father and learned how to judge cattle. Praze Young Farmers brought in breeders to teach us too, and as a member I used to enter stock judging competitions at the various shows. It was piecemeal training but there were no day-release courses then and life on Tregotha gave me lots of opportunities to practice what I'd learned. I was chosen for the county judging team at Smithfield in 1967. Unfortunately there was a nationwide outbreak of foot and mouth disease that year, so the whole event had to be cancelled.

I saw quite a lot of England, taking vegetables to markets in different places and sometimes, buying winter feed in. My father's older brother John had a biggish farm at Wadebridge, thirty miles away, beyond Truro. In winter I'd go up there with Clare Treloar to buy straw from Uncle John and my cousin Martin, who is not much older than me. We had to buy winter feed in because both Uncle Derrick and my Father made good money out of brassicas and broccoli and had no room left for more cereals. Ours had been a dairy herd but we were gradually working the breed standard of South Devons around to beef and dairy.

I suppose I could have gone to an agricultural college, or a university but I never wanted to. All I ever wanted to do was farm, which, like any other endeavour, meant knowing the basics backwards, learning to judge risk, and trusting the right people.

-

My first year of married life was eventful and wonderful. I had both Camborne Rugby fixtures (which made me happy) and Adele at home (who made me happier still). We had a new dog - a sweet-natured English Border Collie puppy called Rex, who arrived warm, furry and safe in a box in the guard's van of a train from Wales. I was Chairman of the Young Farmers and active in agitating for produce grading. Our herdsman, a Yorkshireman called Alan Cook who'd been with us for three or four years, was quick to learn, loyal and a good companion. Our cattle were doing well and Father, as Chairman of the South Devon sales company, flew to America to spread the word. He must have charmed those old farmers out there because a good many South Devons were exported to the States.

Trevaskis was a lovely, south-facing farm with good soil. I really wanted to establish an orchard like the one at Bezurrel, which I'd always admired as a child. Cornwall wasn't Kent, or the Vale of Evesham. I had to recognise that we'd never have acre upon acre of apple-blossom drifting above the hedges in spring. Our county is just too windy. So what I looked hard at, second best for me but still promising, was soft fruit - mainly raspberries and strawberries.

While I was making decisions like these, Serena was born, early one October morning, at the Bolitho Hospital at Penzance. I'd taken Adele in the night before and for some reason, probably because this baby was our first, I'd imagined that our first child would turn up after I'd spent the morning planting cauliflower, rather than when I was still out in the field. I jumped in the car and tore down to Penzance to see them. I'd never held, or even seen, such a tiny human being before and I loved her straight away.

I was back to playing with Camborne Rugby Club that winter, and after a few Wednesday nights training, and a couple of games, I was back in the first team. In the early seventies I could make the time. Serena was an easy baby, and so was Charles George, when he arrived in 1971. The year after, we all went down to Penzance and had a professional take a picture of the Four Georges: George Henry, who was in his late eighties then, George my father, me (George Paul) and the new boy (Charles George) who would always be known by his middle name.

With my father busy with all his business interests, it fell to me to make most of the short-term decisions about Tregotha. Early in '74 Adele was expecting another baby and I was beginning to feel a bit detached from my rugby; I was too preoccupied with the business. That winter was bitter, with snow on the fields, and I remember one Saturday morning saying to my father

'We should get these caulis cut. There's frost forecast. I shouldn't be playing this afternoon.'

'Oh, you go on,' he said. 'The men will manage.'

So I went to Penryn, where we were playing, stood on the wing frozen to the marrow, regretting my decision to be here, and never got a pass all afternoon. That was the decider for me. I could do better for myself, and my business, by working – certainly by being available to work. I gave up the rugby after that.

Giles was born in 1974, dark-haired like Adele, and since both she and I had two siblings each, we decided that three was the perfect number of children to have. When Giles was a few months old, Adele would go out into the fields and work, and take them all with her. With Giles in his carry-cot, the other two could play while she cut cabbage or pulled celery. Mrs James, who worked for us then, would bring toys for them.

Getting to grips with risk and loss

In 1968 I had never been happier; I was marrying Adele Olds at St Buryan's beautiful little church. Even that day, with the bridesmaids and the honeymoon, the dress, the in-laws and the godparents, the reception, and the scores of relations on both sides – Tregotha and its business were very much present in our lives. Among the good wishes from friends at our glorious wedding was a telegram of congratulations signed by Mr Whitt and every member of staff at the bank in Camborne.

That's the kind of relationship we had with the bank in those days. But the National Provincial Bank had already merged with the Westminster, and when we got that telegram the Camborne branch would soon close. From early 1970, Mr Scragg would be our manager at the National Westminster. Fortunately my father, who always had half an eye on his financial commitments, got on with him too.

In '75 we were still taking vegetables up to the Midlands in our Bedford KM lorry. I don't know whether it was the new motorways, or just old age, but the darned thing never stopped giving trouble that year. It kept breaking down and the engine would over-rev so when I finally decided to get a new one, I was determined to get something that would cruise along at 65 miles an hour without steam, smoke or ominous grinding noises. The right thing became available and I could try it out on the Easter Saturday. I went up to Beeston, Nottinghamshire, took a good look and had a drive, and gave them a cheque. I said 'I'll have it. I'll come back and take it on Monday but I'll get a letter from the bank for you so you know it'll go through on Tuesday.'

I knew I'd need a bank transfer so I called Mr Scragg about making the money available immediately after the Bank

Holiday. He promised to call in at Trevaskis tomorrow with the paperwork so that I could pick the lorry up on Monday. At Trevaskis on Easter Sunday we had the whole family, my sisters, brothers-in-law and their families and my mother and father. We always went to their farms at Christmas and they came to us at Easter. This time, we had Mr Scraggs as well. He came out to see us specially and, on the Monday, I was able to drive up with Kelvin Kraze and collect my Guy lorry with a Gardner 180 engine. I drove it home, following Kelvin in my car ahead.

Later, in the seventies, along came a manager called Ken Earl. In those days, 'the branch was the bank'. Its manager (then commonly spelled with a capital M) was a pillar of the community, like the vicar and the doctor. There would be more than one bank in every town but between them they would know and socialise with every significant local business.

Ken Earl and Father just didn't get on. Father didn't get the respect he deserved. He was by nature optimistic, expansive, full of ideas with plenty of drive to make them happen. This new manager would listen to Father, look at the costs of whatever he was suggesting, and get quite panic-stricken.

My father came home shaking his head. 'He's useless. Real old woman. Worried about this, can't do that - can't stay the horses with him at all.'

Then came the day when Earl bounced one of my father's cheques. Father went bright red, marched into the bank and straight through the door marked The Manager, and banged his fist on the desk.

'What the hell d'you think you're doing? You don't stop my bloody payments! Who are you? Who gave you the right to ruin my reputation?'

'Mr Eustice –'

'Don't you *Mr Eustice* me. What are you doing in this job? You don't seem to understand how farming works. You bloody well put that through right now and don't ever do that to me again!'

He stormed out and that night he said to me

'I'm not dealing with that fellow any more. You'll have to talk to him. I can't get on with him at all.'

Earl was the first bad bank manager we ever had, but things calmed down after that. In other ways, Father was essentially satisfied, as people are when they know their business and keep looking ahead. But from then on, I had to talk to the bank.

Long-term policy and expensive changes at Tregotha were Father's decisions, usually after consultation with me and, sometimes, the bank. Vehicles were expensive. Early in 1970 our old Dodge truck came to a sudden and irreversible halt. This was in the middle of a very good season, when we were trucking our vegetables to Wolverhampton, Cardiff, Covent Garden and other places, so Dad had to find us a new lorry fast. He got a Bedford and we put a temporary body on it, unpainted. That summer, when the panic was over, we had it sprayed and got a cattle-box made. We'd expanded the herd and were showing more.

We could go forward now that the business of childbirth was over and child-rearing was under way. My priority was to get on in the farming world. I was always looking for ways to save here, make money there and raise the profile of our farms. I was a probationary South Devon cattle judge, and would go to Judge's Days up in Devon; we'd have to judge South Devons and explain the reasons for our choices to the accredited men. At the same time, I invited the Praze Young Farmers to Trevaskis and would teach them how to judge beef cattle at the summer shows.

I mentally did a time-and-motion study on our vegetable enterprise's packing and transport. All our vegetables had to be cut or pulled (by hand) and carted from field to packing shed. Until a few years back we'd used a horse and cart. The horse would walk on his own and stop when you shouted 'Whoa' and caught up with him, working along the line. You'd chuck vegetables in until he had a full load and then you'd lead him over to the shed and tip the vegetables out for packing and loading. Nowadays, we collected the vegetables by tractor and trailer, with a second tractor and trailer in reserve for busy times. We took them to the packing house, packed them in crates and loaded them onto a lorry for the wholesalers. It was a reasonably neat system; since we were selling in the Midlands, we'd come back laden with wooden crates from the Tewkesbury Box Company. We used small, 16-inch ones because the customers liked them better than great big unwieldy things. I saw that we could speed up the journey from field to shed. At this point we were growing over forty acres of cauliflower alone and I saw that we could save time by packing straight from the field. I'd intuitively mastered the important art of making lots of small changes, which together add up to a better result.

Father was supposed to have given up manual work in '67 but driving agricultural vehicles didn't count. He bought a wider combine harvester, a Fahr M60, and would cut corn with that and haul most of it over to Uncle Derrick, who had a dryer, to make it into straw. Because our herd was now mainly a beef herd they needed plenty of straw for the winter. South Devons were beautiful animals and I worked at my judging. In 1974, at only 28, I was invited to judge at the Royal of England; my father was very proud.

-

If I hadn't been born to farming I probably wouldn't believe the risks involved. For a start there's pests and diseases – things like potato blight or swarms of locusts (which we missed) or Dutch Elm Disease (which devastated a windbreak later). And of course, weather: years like 1976, for instance, when there was a six-month drought and we were trying to pump water up from the river at Tregotha. If there's frost, no frost, rain, no rain, a heatwave, a high wind or floods, a crop or a herd somewhere on this planet will die of it. The farmer will be looking into the black hole of insolvency and the bank will probably put it down to his incompetence.

To this day nobody can give you a reliable weather forecast more than a few days ahead, and in 1978 – forget it. The winter of 78/79 turned out to be among the worst in living memory and we lost almost all our winter vegetables.

So in '79, when I suggested a constructive way to get out of the hole we were in, Ken Earl at the Natwest demanded a forward budget - something I'd never had to produce before, and for which (see above *re:* weather) I could see no rational justification. I had to do it though because I believed in trying a new way ahead. We were over-reliant on winter income but we always had a lot of visitors driving past on the road behind Trevaskis in the summer and I thought if we grew strawberries and raspberries we could advertise them as Pick-Your-Own and generate some cash.

My father was apprehensive but I went right ahead. I planted four acres of strawberries and five of raspberries, and because Uncle Paul Richards from Splattenridden had always grown rhubarb I put a couple of acres of that in as well. If we could harvest it early we would beat the rest of the country to market.

Once we'd done this we all kept quiet about it. One of the fields was close to a road and we noticed other farmers stopping to stick their noses over the hedge because we were growing these plants in a different way from any vegetable they'd ever seen. We told them nothing. The green shoots could have been Triffids, for all they knew; we ignored queries. I didn't want to be pre-empted by local competition.

Meanwhile, back in Camborne, Ken Earl was still scowling about our poor winter vegetable harvest. Feeling anxious he decided to pay us a visit and bring along the bank's agricultural expert for this region. I drove them around the farm, explaining what they saw before them: soft fruit for pick-your-own.

'How much did all this lot cost?' growled Earl.

'Three thousand.'

'Three thousand pounds? You've just lost all those crops, and now you spend more money?'

'Well, we've just lost £30,000, so I thought another three grand wouldn't hurt much.'

He didn't reply. Disapproving, poker-faced. Of course I was being ironic. But how on earth did he think we were ever likely to recover from a loss without somehow trying to make a compensatory gain? He really hadn't a clue how optimistic a farmer has to be. Our wage book for the start of the 78/79 winter had shown us employing seven good knowledgeable workers and a lorry driver; by January, thanks to wind and rain and unseasonable cold, I'd had to lay off four of them and only three farmhands were still working. One of the men who left had been with us for more than a decade.

Strawberries and raspberries take a season to establish and if you're lucky, they'll crop heavily for the next two years. So we planted in March, worked hard and sold what we had to local wholesalers. They did well. That October of '79 Adele and I went to a PYO conference in Solihull to learn as much as we could. We made new friends, exchanged a lot of information, and made some orchard visits as well. In 1980 we launched our own PYO enterprise. We set aside about an acre of land as a car park, enclosed the picking area so that people had to enter and leave by the same entrance, and weighed and sold the fruit from an old shed.

I'd never seen so much cash. That summer we took about £10,000 from strawberries alone. I liked growing new things so I put up a blackboard and invited people to tick a box next to the kinds of fruit they most wanted to pick. I don't think there was a single thing somebody didn't want; gooseberries, blackcurrants, redcurrants, blackberries, loganberries... My father told his friends 'I spent half my life trying to get rid of brambles on the farm and now Paul's putting them in.'

We knew by late summer that we'd done well but Ken Earl was still grumbling. He saw the forward budget. 'Gooseberry planting - £300' was the final straw. I thought we were going to have to sell the furniture. Yet we were not being extravagant. Our lorry took vegetables up to the Midlands and the North and came back with soft fruit from Worcestershire and rhubarb from Cheshire. We also brought straw down from Worcestershire for Uncle Derrick's herd. The gooseberries would make money. Earl, thank goodness, left the Camborne branch around then.

I took George to Fruit Focus that year. It was a big selling exhibition at Writtle, near Chelmsford. We had a long drive and he was only nine. Adele and I had become friendly with a couple in Norfolk who'd been doing PYO much longer than us, and they grew apples, so I decided to do the same. The man from Blackmoor's at Fruit Focus said

'Where you from, then?'

'Cornwall' I replied.

'Oh, well you'll need plenty of windbreaks for your apples then. Have you planted windbreaks already?'

'No. I didn't know I'd need them.'

'You will. Give them two or three years to fill out and then come back and buy your trees.'

I was impatient. I wanted an orchard and I wanted it now. So they said:

'Alright. Go and see this man at Long Ashton. He'll tell you what to do.' They gave me the name of George Gilbert at Long Ashton and thanks to his advice, in March of 1981 we ended up planting a thousand trees of the variety he recommended; and I went to Rosewarne Experimental Station, near here, to see what kind of windbreaks I should use. I planted Alnus Cordata, which they had there. I put in a couple of acres of Victoria and Czar plums as well. The plums gave us a stingy crop for the next decade and never really liked Cornwall much, but the PYO was a huge success. If you know your land, you have to make the best of it.

-

Dad died in the August of 1985, when I was 39. He was only sixty-eight but he was bronchitic, had been since he was sixty at least. He smoked cigarettes, like most men then and, for more than a decade when he was young, he'd worked with a belt-driven threshing machine every harvest, a big noisy whirring old thing that made a chop, chop, chop, chop noise hour after hour, with his men forking the golden wheat up, another man feeding it into the mouth of the hopper, and the grain, with its husks intact, pouring out down a chute into sacks that more men hauled to one side. You ended up with a pile of straw and lungs full of dust. At harvest time my father was threshing day after day, because a lot of farmers didn't have their own machine, and he'd tow his around with a tractor, doing contract work. One day, the fruits of these efforts would pay for my education at Truro Cathedral School. I think the dust helped to kill him though.

He'd had medication and an inhaler for a few years before he was admitted to West Cornwall Hospital in Penzance in the April of '85. While he was there, a salesman we both knew was down from Wolverhampton, so I took him in with me to see my father. The invalid sat up in bed and talked. He and I often held differing views and whoever turned out to be right, over a given argument, always crowed a bit. It was just friendly rivalry and, as farmers, we were more than happy when anything worked. In his own lifetime he had seen the risks associated with growing cauliflowers, or broccoli, as they are called in Cornwall and he had suggested that we abandon growing winter vegetables and focus on the cattle which had lower earning potential but were less risky. He was eating his words now. He had today's paper. 'Look at this,' he said to me and the salesman. There was a headline 'Green Gold' and the story was all about the high price of greens. We'd now been growing cauliflower broccoli since the beginning but they had rarely made us any money in the previous ten years. This year, at last, they very much did. Dad had always said

'You want to concentrate on the cattle, boy. Those winter veg are too up and down.'

Being go-ahead and determined, and now, vindicated, I expected more years like 1985. Needless to say, there was never a day after that – far less a season – that ever came close to it. But I was always an optimist. Like my father, I saw us going from strength to strength, whatever problems we might have to surmount on the way. When he died, I would be the latest beneficiary in a line of five eldest sons going back a hundred and fifty years. I now had two sons of my own. My dream was that one day, George would take Tregotha and Giles would take Bezurrel.

My Dad talked knowledgeably about cattle and growing crops, especially vegetables; he was shrewd about people and intelligent about driving his business forward. He was a terrific father and spent a lot of time with me. He never talked much in depth about his money. With hindsight I wish he had.

When he came home that summer he seemed much better. He started doing what he'd done before, going to shows and attending meetings as a director. He held directorships at Grenville Motors (where he was the Chairman), Gwinear Farmers (where his father George Henry had been a founding member), Tyack's and Rice's the Ironmongers, Tonkins Bakers, West Cornwall Meat Traders, and the Royal Cornwall Show at Wadebridge, which he went to that July. He'd been at a meeting in Camborne on the Saturday, 17th of August, before he got very ill in the night and our mother had to call the doctor, who called for an ambulance to take him back to the hospital. I got there as he was being manoeuvred downstairs strapped to a stretcher. 'Ah there you are,' he murmured. 'hand me those fags on the mantelpiece will you?'

'I'll bring them in when I come over' I said, well knowing that hospitals didn't allow you to puff away at a packet of Weights in your hospital bed. My sister Catherine and I went to see him that evening and he was much improved, better than he'd been before. I didn't take the cigarettes in, but he had rallied, and didn't seem to mind.

Next morning, Monday, the hospital called. We needed to go back because Dad was 'very poorly', they said. Our mother chose not to go and I set off by myself.

As I drove past Gwinear Church the bells were ringing; a great soaring peal and a jangling fall, over and over. I had never heard them on a Monday morning before, and I was unnerved. Dad had set up the fund and raised the money for those bells. I told myself the ringers must be visitors. There are always tourists in Cornwall in August and bell-ringers among them like to knock at the vicarage door and ask permission to exercise the bells for half an hour. But it was so strange, so poignant somehow.

I can't remember whether or not Mary got to the West Cornwall Hospital in time, but Catherine and I were too late. Dad had died. We were horribly upset. He'd seemed invincible. We were not ready for him to leave us.

The next day, we gathered in the kitchen at Tregotha to discuss the funeral arrangements. At some point the inevitable question arose.

'Is there a will?'

Our mother shook her head. 'No I don't think he ever made one.'

'I don't think he ever got round to it. He didn't want to face it. He didn't know what to do.'

My father had always hoped to get into a position where he could leave some property to all of his children but all of the farms had been bought on borrowed money and the deeds for every farm were held by the bank as security. Even the deeds for Tregotha Farm had been passed over as security some time before I joined the business.

My father's funeral was a huge affair. He had been christened at Gwinear Church, and so had Catherine, Mary and I. It is an ancient place, most of it between five and eight hundred years old, which has witnessed many a Eustice baptism, marriage and burial.

Every farmer and show judge and farm supplier and customer for miles around knew George Eustice, and from distant parts as well; he had traded with people all over England. Gwinear Church couldn't hold the crush. There were five hundred mourners at least, and scores of them had to stand in the churchyard throughout the service. Cars lined the lanes and were pulled up on verges all over the village. Cecil Olds, my father-in-law, told me he'd never been to a funeral as big as this.

In the following months, our attention turned to resolving the estate. Mostly, my father's estate was owned by G. Eustice & Son, in which my mother and I were the only remaining partners but there was a significant level of debt attached to it and all of the farms were offered to the bank as security. The partnership had also granted a tenancy over Tregotha, in my favour, to secure tenure of the farm for the long term and for tax planning purposes. The Tregotha tenancy was to assume a much greater significance a decade later as we fought Barclays Bank.

The value of my father's estate, after taking account of borrowing, was ninety thousand pounds. When a married man dies intestate half his property goes to the widow and the other half must be divided equally between the children. I think it came as something of a surprise to my two sisters that there were significant debts attached to the farms. I had grown used to it having been in the business for some time and having seen both the investments, the risks and the difficult years that had contributed to it. In the end, we all sat at the kitchen table in Tregotha with a land agent who suggested that I should buy out Mary and Catherine.

My father had come from a generation where business was kept very private, even from family. At times I wondered whether it might have been far easier for all of us if he had made a will. However, I also completely understood why he felt too constrained to be able to do so. There were hopes and expectations that he would have wanted to deliver on but which he knew he couldn't. Although working through this situation was difficult for my sisters and I, we all dealt with matters in a constructive way and brought things to a conclusion that kept the farms together.

-

In the January after Dad died, I celebrated my fortieth birthday. In public, I was a farmer, stockbreeder and grower who owned a significant amount of land, and exploited it to its maximum potential pioneering new ways of doing things such as selling directly to the public. In private, we ran a very highly geared business that needed to innovate and outperform norms in order to meet finance costs.

The *West Briton* barely noticed something called Big Bang. You couldn't avoid it on the BBC, in 1986. If you'd asked me what it was, I'd probably have said it was something about finance in London. The rules about stockbrokers were changing. But stockbrokers in the City were, as far as I knew, complacent fellows mainly found on golf courses and catching a train home to Surrey at three o'clock after a long lunch. Their goings-on wouldn't affect us down in Cornwall so why would I care?

I didn't have a crystal ball but if I had, I might have paid more attention because when financial market regulations changed in October '86, and the high-street banks bought up merchant banks and brokers, they got mean and lean. The long lunches stopped, the long days started, and the lazy old buffers dropped out. The new generation of financial managers had worked in Hong Kong and Singapore and New York. They employed sharp people and expert technology. A computer would give them a rigid, hard-headed answer. It didn't judge a man by his character.

These focussed attitudes and systems also came to prevail in their associated retail banks, the so-called 'Big Four' that cleared our cheques amongst themselves - the National Westminster, Barclays, the Midland and Lloyds. These clearing banks operated out of thousands of small-town branches that dealt with people like us. They grew more sophisticated and faster thanks to computers in the back office, and began incentivising their staff to maximise profit. Those profits became available to their own associated investment banks, which meant the whole London financial system mushroomed on a flood-tide of ordinary-people's-money. Advertising, debit cards and computerised salary payments encouraged the unbanked half of the population to open accounts. In the branches, counter staff weren't clerks any more but salespeople, actively selling products – insurance, mortgages, loans. Preliminary decisions were churned out by computers designed to credit-score loan applications regardless of the 'I remember your father' factor.

Banks were always bureaucratic. How could they be anything else? But in the new reformed hierarchy of grades, branch managers lost much of the autonomy, and status, they'd once had. Anything remotely risky had to be referred up to a Regional HQ. Thousands of middle-aged men who'd risen to Manager would go no further. In the past, they'd have stayed in the same branch, guiding the financial fortunes of prominent local families, until they retired. Now they were shuffled off out of sight - often 'seconded' in their forties to a good cause, before being offered early retirement.

This new culture took a few years to arrive in Camborne and I was unaware of it for a long time. Back in '86, when it was just beginning, all I noticed was the new demand on my resources. No sooner had I paid nearly £30,000 to my sisters than the Inland Revenue had noticed our stellar profits from cauliflower in the year 1985 to '86. I had to find about £40,000 in tax at the end of the year.

Ray Plummer had succeeded Windy Ken Earl at the bank, and to please him and get my overdraft down I sold about thirty cattle at Gloucester Market through Bruton Knowles. I knew Ray through his brother Kenny, like me a Rugby player and runner. Ray was understanding about my outstanding overdraft, and the situation I found myself in after my father's death. I remember walking round Trevaskis with him and explaining why I'd always talked to Bob Seymour, the assistant manager, rather than Ken. 'That's all over now,' he said cheerfully as he left. 'From now on you can deal with me.' He was truly supportive.

Soon after my father died we had to give up thirty acres that had been making money for us for more than twenty years. The tenancy of Penbroath Farm, a bit closer to Camborne at Carnhell Green, ended with my father's death and wasn't renewed.

I regretted that. I remembered when we'd first got it. I'd have been about seventeen then. The farmer had retired but he wanted to live in the house and get an income from the land. Under the terms of the tenancy, no vegetables could be grown, only grass or corn. My father agreed to that, with reluctance, but came to regret it. Our first year there was dismal. We planted barley on two fields, about ten acres altogether. We had a bagger combine and a three tonne wood trailer and from those two fields, we recovered one load of straw and one load of barley.

'This is no good. We're not getting any production from this place.'

Father saw that the fields were neglected and needed tender care. He finally persuaded the farmer to let us grow brassicas to help recondition the soil and we were able to get out and plough up some of the grass for cauliflowers. We had a three-row multi-planter at the time and Clare Treloar drove it while three of us sat on the back planting – me, Kenny Hollow and Maureen, Ken's wife. All that work proved to be a waste of time too, as it soon became apparent that nothing would grow there. The ground was full of wireworm. We had to dip the plants and re-plant.

We struggled for a couple of years to get those thirty acres back into a growing condition but, thanks to us, for decades afterwards, Penbroath Farm would grow anything. So when my father died, and I had to give it up, I admit I was a bit piqued that after all that effort, the farm in 1987 was good for someone else to farm.

Fortunately for me, two useful plots of land became available to buy. The year after Father died I bought Lemin Farm, just 33 acres, and in 1987 I added Trenawin – twenty acres and some buildings adjoining Trevaskis.

Lemin was of special interest because it was where my grandmother Katy Eustice had been brought up. Her family had owned it and after her father's death, Lemin Farm - which was about a hundred acres altogether - ended up divided in two between two cousins of my father, Alec and Jim Rowe. Alec had sold up to a Mr Noy, who was now selling his half. So when an agent rang me to tell me the land was on the market, I immediately considered Jim Rowe.

'What about Jim?' I said. 'Would he want it?'

'No, he wouldn't want that.'

I thought I should keep it in the family, and I needed extra land, so in 1987 I went to see Ray Plummer at the NatWest Bank and he was positive. I was able to buy it.

I had learned to farm independently, although my father had always been there, somebody I could consult if I was in doubt, and I missed him; whether or not I took his advice, I valued it. Adele and I were on our own now. Opportunities were coming my way, and I was increasing my turnover.

I needed help at Tregotha and Derrick wanted hands at Bezurrel but that was all right because at Trevaskis and Tregotha we had people who'd always worked for us. They knew the fields and the stock and the knack of starting any temperamental equipment as well as I did. I had Alan Cook, who was always loyal and trustworthy, looking after the livestock. Because I'd sold quite a few of the cattle, I had to find extra work for Alan but he didn't mind at all working on the vegetable crops as well. He used to do a lot of the field packing and planting and tractor-driving. Anthony Mitchell, who lived in the other farmhouse at Angarrack Hill farm, was the main tractor driver. John Eddy was our lorry driver and, in the summer months, turned his hand to driving the broccoli planter and tractor driving. I used to work with the broccoli cutting gang in the winter, and Adele would work with the spring green gang. She used to cut the spring greens mostly with Pam Cook, Alan's wife, who worked in the fields. So did Anthony's wife Sue. I also had Kevin Keen, Antony Mitchell and Paul Blewett.

I wanted to increase the size of our herd, but with 250 acres already in production, I had nowhere to graze any more cattle. I couldn't buy any more land – I'd only just taken on two new pieces – but I decided that if I could rent some, I'd move the herd onto it and increase the amount of vegetables we were growing at Tregotha, Trevaskis and Angarrack Hill. In the *West Briton* I saw an advertisement for 100 acres to rent at Kehelland Farm. When I rang I found it belonged to Colin and Avril Benney, who were related to me, and it had been tenanted by a farmer I knew. It wasn't in great shape but I was prepared to make improvements.

The first year I had that extra hundred acres, we cut hay there and brought it back to our barns at Tregotha, Trevaskis and Lemin. We didn't have to make so much silage that year and it allowed us to be able to plant more vegetables.

All the same, it didn't produce the crop it should. I persuaded Colin Benney to let me plough some of the fields and crop them with winter cauliflowers for two years, and then to reseed the fields again to improve the quality of the grassland. It was lime-deficient, among other things, so we would plough the fields and then lime them and have two crops of winter cauliflower, and then seed them back into grassland again after a crop of barley.

This allowed me to increase the vegetable growing acreage quite considerably. Within a few years we were growing around 80 acres of winter cauliflowers and 40-odd acres of spring greens. The increased acreage sometimes meant 12-hour days, harvesting and planting at weekends and evenings as well. But we had great people, our turnover was improving and prices were good.

I wanted to change the way we harvested the vegetables. Other growers were moving to cutting rigs: you'd cut the cauliflower and drop it into the cup of a boom that projected from one side of a tractor, and it would be conveyed up to the packers on the same machine.

Our old cutting system, which I had designed, had been good for about fifteen years but we needed to cope with larger acreage now. That summer, at the Royal Cornwall Show, I bought a Belarus high-clearance four-wheel-drive tractor, which would suit perfectly. I even used it for cutting the hay at Kehelland and, once harvest was over I got the local David

Brown dealer to help make it into a cutting rig for our winter picking. Kelvin Kraze helped me install one forklift at the back and another on the front so that we could carry a couple of wooden bins each end. At the end of a row we could fork-lift them directly onto the trailer and from there to the lorry for transport to the markets. That saved us an immense amount of handling, and it was a system that we used for a further ten years.

All the fertilizers and cattle feed and other necessities, from petrol for the vehicles to baler twine, we got from Gwinear Farmers. My grandfather George Henry had been a founding partner of Gwinear & District Farmers in 1918 so, despite tempting offers from elsewhere, I remained a loyal customer – to the extent of spending about £60,000 a year with them. In 1988 I even became the Chairman of their Committee.

The summer of '88 was better than ever for Pick Your Own. Our apple trees had flourished, thanks to the windbreaks, and we were getting excellent crops from all our soft fruit and thousands of visitors over the season. Many of these people wanted a cup of tea and would have to drive into Camborne or St Ives, or straight home, to get one. So Adele said:

'We need to have a tea-room. I could do afternoon teas. Make more of a day out for people.'

'Good idea. But what'll that cost to build? I'll have to talk to the bank.'

'No, this is my thing. You get on with the farming, you've got enough to do. I'll get some quotes for the price and talk to the bank. I'll set up a special account for it. I'm going to put it in my name. That way it won't affect the main business at all.'

Well, she'd certainly thought it through and she did exactly what she said. Bob Seymour helped her with the business plan and Ray Plummer agreed to let her borrow up to £20,000.

'Tell you what you need to do as well,' he said. 'You're going to have cars parking there, aren't you? The way they do now, near the shop? Well, you want to ask Paul to make an acre or two over to you so that you've always got it as part of your café. You might want to expand, and someday you might want to sell the business, and whoever takes it on will need a bit of land round for a car park and deliveries and so on. Without access rights, the business won't have half the value it should have.'

It was good advice, and I willingly made about an acre over to Adele, little knowing how very important that decision was going to be.

She got planning permission, had the tea-room built out of wood in rustic style, and set it up near the farm shop where people came and left with the fruit they'd picked.

It was all properly kitted out and filled with tables and chairs. Adele and her friend Liz (my cousin, and a very good cook) – the two of them spent hours baking cakes and scones, and we opened to the public.

Not a soul came through the door for three days. Adele was in bits. Then suddenly, maybe thanks to the Cornish bush telegraph, people started coming in and went on doing so for the rest of the season.

The tea-room looked so inviting and well built that the old farm shop was shabby by comparison. I decided to improve it. I set aside the money from an insurance claim I'd made the previous winter. There'd been a big shed at Lemin Farm full of hay and straw. I'd got a man to cover it with galvanised sheeting down to the ground, but a fellow he had working for him began welding next to the straw so of course the whole thing went up in flames – we could see it from a mile away. In due course I got the compensation cheque, but by then I'd decided I didn't need a shed over there anyway. So the money was used to improve the farm shop. The shop and café together were quite an attraction in summer.

I needed more apples for Pick Your Own so I decided to make another orchard over at Trenawin, in a part that was reclaimed land. So the Pick Your Own, the tea room, and the farm shop were doing extremely well every summer, and my debt to the bank was gently shrinking over time. We built a chiller for our beef. I learned the essentials of butchery from a Camborne butcher, and he did very well for us, selling South Devon beef in the farm shop.

Uncle Derrick was having a rough time at Bezurrel in the late 1980s. These were not great times for farming. I thought the main trouble was his health. He had arthritis, and Bezurrel was a big farm, 200 acres.

I had George working with me from 1987. He got eight good O levels but left school at sixteen, and joined Praze Young Farmers as I had. He did all the courses I'd done there and was outstanding at debating and public speaking. He and his friend Robert won the national marketing competition at the Royal Show in '87 and again in '88. That year he made a presentation on South Devons as a beef breed and Robert did the practical butchery.

George saw, as I did, that although we were making a higher profit margin on what we were doing with the Farm Shop and the PYO, that kind of business came along with a lot more financial complexity and we needed to track finances more closely than we would have done in the past. George was also interested in business and had been trading the stock market since he was about 15 and so learned about accounts and the ups and downs of business from a young age. He was already helping with the accountancy side of the restaurant, so to give himself a proper grounding he took a day-release BTech course in Business Studies at Cornwall College.

Most days he carried on learning, as I had, by doing – everything from tractor driving and basic mechanics to planting and harvesting and animal husbandry. We were farming about 350 acres by now. It was starting to feel like a big 'small business', but an efficient one; I'd always invested in good equipment and replaced out of date vehicles with plenty of forethought and regular maintenance. In all my years of farming I think I only ever had one combine that was repeatedly unreliable. We needed machinery and transport that worked because without efficient planting and cutting and baling and driving we wouldn't have a business. In the late eighties I'd often spent a day cutting vegetables, get something to eat and drive the whole lot up to the Midlands, where I'd unload in Wolverhampton and Birmingham. The next day, I'd drive back - usually bringing a load of straw with me – and get to work in the fields again.

I'd driven £29,000 worth of vegetables up to our buyer in Birmingham when his firm folded. That must have been about 1990. I don't know what went wrong, but Receivers went in and ten years later, when they finally wound it up, the creditors got a penny in the pound. We had a cheque for £290 and they had £100,000 in administration fees.

That man from Birmingham had a bungalow down near us. I'd see him around and he'd always promise to make sure I got my money somehow, even if he had to sell the bungalow. He never paid a penny, and then he died. The bungalow turned out to have belonged to his daughter anyway.

Giles left school with six O levels and, like his brother, wanted to come and farm. So he worked with me and studied one day a week at college in Camborne. He was more of a tearaway than his brother. He passed his driving test and had a little Renault sports car. He had friends over at the Lizard, and he stayed the night there sometimes. One morning we were just getting up when the phone rang.

'Mum?' Giles said. 'I've had a bit of an accident. I'm at the Pascoes at Pengwedna. I'm walking back, can you meet me?'

'Are you all right?'

'Yes I'm fine.'

'What kind of accident?'

'Oh, I'll tell you when I see you. I've got to go. Bye – '

By the time Adele was ready to leave we'd talked to Iris Pascoe.

'Well,' she said 'he flew right off the road and turned over in mid-air two or three times - he landed on our field, but there's a big limb down off one of the trees. Must'a been going a hell of a clip.'

We went cold when we heard this.

'So is he really all right?'

'Seems to be. We saw the car and we ran out and he was just climbing up out of it, all smiles, 'Don't worry' he said 'I'm fine - I'll call a garage, I'll get it out of the way- ' and I was so angry with him, but relieved, you know, and I said 'What d'you think you're doing? What kind of driving's that? You need to go back home *this minute* and tell your father or I shall tell him for you.'

So he went in and made his call and started walking. We found him and drove him home. His car we collected later.

There was a bit of an atmosphere at Trevaskis for a while after that.

-

Serena was crazy about horses and she'd ridden a pony, and later a horse, throughout her schooldays. She missed riding and showing and caring for it so much when she went to the University of Kent that we found a field outside Canterbury and took her horse up to live over there. She was the academic one. When she graduated with a 2:1 in microbiology in 1990 she went to work as an agronomist for Shearing Agriculture in Nottingham.

George, having got his BTech in Business Studies, decided to study horticulture full time. We looked at Harper Adams but it was Writtle that he took to. Oddly, this was the very place we'd been to about ten years before, when he was only nine and Adele and I were looking at Pick Your Own for the first time. I reminded him how he'd been so tired at the end of that day that he fell asleep in a café at a service station.

He learned a lot at Writtle, where he did a two-year course plus a year on a fruit farm in Worcestershire. But by then, he was quite involved with things at home; which were not going as well as they should.

Little grey clouds

Britain was officially in recession throughout 1990 and 1991, following a slow decline from about 1988 and an even slower recovery. It didn't affect Trevaskis and Tregotha much, since people still have to eat. Anyway, there was a lot of fat on our business; we had land and property, livestock and deadstock and crops in the ground that were worth a whole lot more than the bank had lent us.

In the late 1980s Uncle Derrick still had arthritis, but seemed otherwise fine. He and Dorothy, and two of their grown-up daughters, had 220 acres of land, a big solid farmhouse, well-built outbuildings, cattle and pigs and he was growing vegetables.

David Vague, my uncle's bank manager at Barclays, was the kindly, fatherly, type of an earlier generation of bank managers where there was more trust placed in the judgement of a local manager.   Like all of us around that time, the pressures on farming incomes and prices coupled with high interest rates had created pressures.

Derrick had submitted plans for a well designed scheme for a modest housing development, a communal green and children's playground on seven acres at Gwinear Field close to Gwinear Village. His application got stopped at every turn by the Planning Committee of West Penwith Council.

He got Bezurrel valued around then. He offered it to me first, and told me he was retiring. 'This farm belongs to you really,' he said. 'It should be inherited in the male line.' But the price was £500,000 which was miles out of my reach. I'd got our overdraft down since Father's death but I'd recently bought land and I still owed about £300,000. I wanted Bezurrel, of course – it had been in the family for many generations – but even if I'd had a hope of finding a lender, I wasn't about to saddle myself and my family with a further half million pound debt.

Uncle Derrick tried to sell but there were no takers. Britain remained badly hit by recession. Town people didn't want a remote farmhouse. No local farmer could afford to buy and run a farm that size.   Months went by, then a year, and he'd sold his cattle.

One day I told Derrick that we needed better pork for the farm shop. We had sausages and pork from my friend the butcher in Camborne, but it was from hybrid pigs and never as good as the British Lop pork from Bezurrel.

'Well,' he said 'Can't help you there. I'm getting rid of the pigs.'

'You never are! Your father started with those. He had them way back, before 1900 didn't he? That's near on a hundred years.'

'Well it may be,' he said 'but I can't make any money out of them. You want to 'ave em?'

'I want to buy the meat,' I said. 'I don't want to run a piggery. Tell you what, I'll pay their keep and buy the carcasses if you keep them at Bezurrel.' So we did that and with the pigs came a little show trailer to hook up behind a car. Alan Cook used to load up two or three pigs, whatever we needed, and tow them to JV Richards' slaughterhouse, and then we'd have the carcasses to cut up for pork and sausages in the shop. Derek had looked after pigs all his life, and there's not a lot of heavy work involved, so he could manage it.

But still nobody wanted agricultural land and you could barely give farmhouses away. Uncle Derrick lowered the price but nobody made a serious offer even then.

It was a good summer for us, 1992, and Adele and I drove up to Taunton one day to visit to a Pick Your Own place. I'd joined Somerset Fruit Growers and they organised these tours and talks for members. We usually learned something from them.

At that time, George was at Writtle College but Alan and Giles and I had been showing our cattle at all the shows and doing very well indeed, particularly with a magnificent bull we had, called Tregotha Concorde, who had recently taken over as sire of the herd from Tregotha Trump the Second, another champion bull. Concorde got his name at the moment of his birth. I was out in the cowshed with Alan attending to a cow in labour when we heard, from above the clouds, a sonic boom, like a thunderclap. It was Concorde, the supersonic plane, shooting overhead as our new calf tumbled onto the straw.

We didn't show Tregotha Concorde as a young bull. We waited until he had matured enough because we knew he was going to be big, and he was a slow developer. But in 1992 we took him to the Royal Cornwall Show, the Three Counties, the Bath and West and the Royal of England. And with Adele still in hospital, at the Royal of England Show at Stoneleigh, he won the South Devon Supreme Championship and South Devon Bull of the Year. This was a marvellous accolade for Tregotha and especially for Alan Cook, our herdsman, who had given so much of his time to the South Devons and prepared them and reared them for the shows.

But I had to rush back to see Adele because they'd finally come up with a diagnosis. They decided that the 'mystery virus' was reactive arthritis. There happened to be a doctor at the hospital who'd worked in Africa and had seen a lot of it there. It's an auto-immune disease, but they began treating her for it, and she slowly got well.

Back at Gwinear, after yet another hoped-for Bezurrel buyer had failed to come across, Uncle Derrick talked to me again.

'You should have Bezurrel, Paul. It belongs to you and the family.'

'You know I'd love to. It's been my dream that one of the boys might take on Tregotha and if the other one could take Bezurrel, we'd keep Trevaskis, and it'd be three farms working together. You know I want your farm, never think I don't, but I'd need strawberries from here to St Ives before I could find five hundred thousand. I can't even look at it.'

'It's come down a lot from what it was Paul. The cattle are gone, and it is time for me to retire. In round figures its about to go on the market at three hundred thousand.'

'Wow, that's quite a drop.'

'Think about it, boy.'

I tried to sleep but couldn't stop thinking about Derrick's offer. Bezurrel Farm was where things had started with my Great Great Grandfather 130 years earlier. Both Derrick and I had a passion for our parish and the farms that our family had nurtured for generations. We both shared a strong desire to keep this land under the custodianship of the Eustice Family.

I had made choices in farming life that hadn't worked out but I always learned something. The few decisions I regretted were the chances I failed to take, which (with hindsight) would have come good. And this was probably the only opportunity I would ever have to buy the original family farm. It was good land and we could restore it and make it pay. But I'd never raise a mortgage for £300,000.

There must be some way out of this.

We didn't need the farmhouse. I never think houses are worth a bag of beans against land. You can always build another house, but you can't magic up some land. We had Angarrack Hill farmhouse, with Anthony Mitchell our main tractor man in it, the main house at Tregotha where my mother lived and then there was Trevaskis; that gave us three good houses already, and Alan Cook's cottage at Tregotha made another one. I might be able to negotiate something about Bezurrel farmhouse with Derrick. I would talk to Adele about it.

It was a Saturday afternoon, visiting time. I sat by the hospital bed and told Adele what Derrick had told me and how I didn't know what to do.

'It's a big decision,' I said 'but what if I could get the land without the house? We could make more off that land than Derrick does and look what it would give us.'

'You mean Derrick and Aunty Dorothy could sell their house?'

'That's what I was thinking.'

'They'd have enough to buy a house in Hayle.'

'Exactly.'

'You really want this, don't you?'

'Of course. I don't know what Ray Plummer'll say though.'

'Paul, don't think twice. If you don't ask you don't get.'

Ray Plummer had become a friend. I should explore it with him. But first of all, I had to get that price down.

1992 had been an excellent summer. We were getting a good seasonal income off the Pick Your Own and the shop, which both showed high profit margins. We were largely able to supply the Farm Shop ourselves. I'd done a course so that we could slaughter our own livestock on the farm, and we were even growing potatoes again now. We were lucky enough to have trustworthy staff and three strong, clever, kind children.

The boys' birthdays were in September, and not far apart, so they invited their friends and we gave them one enormous party in the marquee in front of the restaurant. My mother came, and Mrs Hawkins who'd baby-sat for us for years. She was 85 now and enjoyed the whole evening. We did all the catering, all our wonderful staff were there and I presented Alan Cook with a watch and a painted photograph of South Devons drinking by the water. He'd been with us for 25 years.

Before I saw Ray at the bank, I had another talk with Uncle Derrick. He knew I was interested. I told him I could probably raise £200,000, but no more.

'I don't really want the house at Bezurrel, you see, Uncle Derrick. We've got four already. Why don't you sell that separately?'

It was the family home, built by my great great grandfather. Derrick and my father and my uncle John and all their sisters had been born and brought up in it.

'Tell you what,' he said. 'If you'd buy even just the land, you know, for £200,000, then Dorothy and I can stay on in the house until one of your boys gets married and needs to live in it.'

'We'd like that. You'd be there to keep an eye on the land for us. And would you still look after the pigs?'

'Course I would. The pigs must stay.'

He was such a kind, decent man.

Anyway, he and I had arrived at a solution that worked for both of us. I just hoped it would work for Ray Plummer. I would be paying, effectively, around £1,000 an acre. At the time, that was good value, because Bezurrel land was pretty good and almost all of it was productive. I had to sit down and work out the figures and come up with a package that'd have the Natwest saying yes.

I took advice from Kelsall Steele and talked to John Battell, our solicitor, as well. My forward budget explained that I needed the money to purchase the land at Bezurrel and we'd farm it to its maximum potential as Uncle Derrick had in the past, with South Devons, British Lops and winter vegetables. I gave it to Ray and he liked it but said the most that he at the Camborne branch could lend was, I think, £70,000. Anything more had to be referred up to the regional office, where the Bank employed expert agricultural advisers.

He sent in my application and the paperwork and I got a letter from him. They'd refused – 'were not prepared to extend my borrowings any further'.

I called him.

'What exactly did they say?'

'It's just that it's the wrong time, Paul. They're very tight on lending for agricultural land at the moment.'

I was disappointed because it was autumn of '92 now and I'd made my mind up to have the farm. If Derrick absolutely had to sell, then I supposed Bezurrel house and farm together would go to auction with a low reserve price. Without money behind me I wouldn't even be able to bid for it. I needed to take the opportunity to buy while it was possible.

I discussed it all with Giles and George and we came up with a better idea. George, who was good with figures, was working at Bransford Nurseries, in Worcestershire, in the final months of his degree in horticulture, but we got together when we could at a half way point – a service station on the motorway – to refine our new proposal. We knew that we could grow strawberries earlier than the rest of the country; they'd been profitable for us for more than a decade and Bezurrel's south-facing fields would be ideal.

So we got Mike Ryan, the ADAS strawberry expert, to come and look at what we wanted to do. He saw the land at Bezurrel and everything else we were doing and maybe our optimism was infectious, but he liked it so much that he asked Douglas Kemp from Kentish Garden to come and talk to us. Kentish Garden was a marketing organisation for soft fruit growers and he was as excited by our plans as Mike had been.

So we went back to Ray with a revised, and stronger, Farm Plan, explaining everything right down to the varieties we proposed to plant at Bezurrel.

Ray was more hopeful this time, but again the regional office wouldn't buy it, or to be accurate, they might if we gave them agricultural charges over our business. That was the equivalent of a no, because agricultural charges are to be avoided at all costs. They give a bank the right to seize your crop, including crops in the ground, and livestock. They make your land valueless to anyone else, including any alternative sources of finance.

We were racking our brains when Uncle Derrick pointed out that Barclays was his bank and maybe they would look at our application. He'd introduce us to his bank manager.

So George and Giles and Derrick and I went to see David Vague, a nice old fellow, at the Camborne Barclays. He was pleased to see us; very pleased. He was receptive to our arguments about extending the farmland for family reasons and when we described our proposal in detail he thought it sounded promising. But since the Camborne branch had a limited lending capacity, he would have to consult somebody 'at Local Director level.' He left the room to make a phone call. When he came back he told us

'They'll take a look at it. No promises mind.'

My sons and I set about refining the plans one more time. We wanted to be sure that the forward budgets and farm plan were totally practical and realistic and accurately reflected what we wanted to do. Strawberries are a triennial crop, as we pointed out; the first year's harvest is relatively weak compared to the next two, and then you leave the land for a year before replanting.

We put our proposal together and submitted it for a third time. 'If they like it in principle, they'll want to send somebody down to have a look at the farm,' David Vague said. He put it forward to 'them' and we waited.

A helping hand to Barclays Bank

One day in October 1992 David Vague brought Bruce Hammond to see us. He was the Barclays manager for agriculture, South West Region, based in Exeter; a burly, untidy fellow, but cheerful. I showed them over the farm at Bezurrel, which they'd both seen before, and after that I drove them around the rest of the land we farmed. Hammond saw it all, from the houses to the livestock and even the farm shop. It was late morning when I pulled into the car park outside Adele's restaurant. They'd both been invited to lunch there.

We had an informal discussion there and then, before we even got out of the car.

Hammond seemed to like what we were doing. Then David Vague said

'Paul, you know if we're going to take this forward then we'll want to be your sole bankers.'

'What d'you mean?'

'Well, at the moment of course you're trading as G Eustice & Son, in partnership with your mother, and we'd like G Eustice & Son to bank with us.'

'Oh I don't want to move from our bank. I'm only asking for the money for Bezurrel.'

'You see, the Local Directors would approach an application such as yours more favourably if it came from, so to speak, a known quantity.'

I'd thought we were a known quantity now that they'd seen our thriving business, but it seemed they also wanted to oversee our trade as it happened, far into the future.

I didn't want to leave Natwest. Ray had progressed our business to my satisfaction and Bob Seymour had been a friend for years now. I'd be mortified if I seemed disloyal.

So I didn't like this. All I said was 'I don't know. I don't think that'll work at all. I'll discuss it with the family.'

'That's the other thing, you see. Adele's business is with the Natwest, isn't it? It would make a much neater proposition if she moved her restaurant over to us as well.'

'Why would she want to do that?'

'Well let's discuss it with her. She's doing very well isn't she? We may be able to offer a more favourable rate than she's getting.'

Adele, and George, and Giles were all going to be affected by all this so as soon as we could, we had a long talk. My mother always said 'you just go ahead, Paul. I'll be guided by you' when it came to G. Eustice & Son. She'd sign whatever I thought was best.

In the end, we decided to go ahead and move all our business over to Barclays. Adele came along too. I told Bruce Hammond

'We're prepared to move everything over to you. You're supporting me, so we'll be prepared to support you.'

After all, the Natwest had let us down. So I justified what I still saw as my own disloyalty on grounds of fair dealing with a benefactor. At that point I didn't see the bank as rapacious, but as benevolent and generous; paternalistic, I suppose. We'd always used our overdraft cautiously, never without clear intent to expand or improve and increase turnover. I didn't dare imagine a worst-case scenario in which Barclays, once they had all our business, might arbitrarily decide to take it away from us.

A day or two later David Vague called to reassure me.

'When we were driving over to you, you know what, Bruce Hammond said you didn't stand a snowball in hell's chance of getting your proposal accepted. And then after, when you'd shown him the farms and the way you're managing them, and he'd met you and George, when we were driving back here he said you'd got one of the most promising plans he'd ever seen. He thought you were all very capable and what he liked about the plan was that if the worst happened, and the crop got ruined by weather, yes your returns would go down, but so would your labour and input costs.'

We were not yet through with the banking formalities when David Vague reappeared at Trevaskis along with Trevor Furse, the Manager from Truro who would be looking after the account because it would be too big for the Camborne branch. He wanted to look at Tregotha, Trevaskis, Angarrack Hill and the other land we owned. Together with Bezurrel and some rented land it would be over 500 acres. Furse knew our family by repute. He'd even heard about the South Devons. I assumed he'd seen the farm plan, and understood it. He listened anyway as I explained the implications, irrigation costs and three-year cycle, and so on, of the strawberry project.

Maybe I have a tendency to underestimate how little townspeople know about farming. Bank managers, for instance, will have passed exams in banking, and have picked up information about other trades in the course of their job. I don't think Furse was an expert, although he did say he was impressed by the way we were running everything, and he got that right. The farmers who failed were usually the ones who were stuck in old-fashioned ways, and we were among the pioneers in Cornwall with our soft fruit and orchards, our Pick-Your-Own, the farm shop and the restaurant.

We had an amicable lunch together, and discussed moving the accounts. Now that the deal was getting closer I was facing my innermost suspicions. We'd always run everything off an overdraft with the Natwest and now we'd be working with a big secured loan as well and I said

'You know ...this is a very big thing we're talking about. If we're giving you control over all our debt, there are implications. You've got a lot of power. You could take it all from us. What if you just want our farms? We could end up with nothing.'

'That won't happen. Why would it? I don't think we'd be very popular in this part of the world if we put the Eustices out of business. It's in our interests to see you prosper, as Cornish farmers. You're a significant part of the local economy.'

That was true. In any case, what would they gain by winding us up? I knew of no demand for our land from property developers or mining companies or anyone else, and as for farmers, our expertise right here, in a patch of Cornwall three miles by three, had been refined over generations. We'd have good and bad years, as is normal, but as long as the land stayed in our hands, only an Act of God could make a dead loss of it.

So we had a meeting at Trevaskis, in the dining room, that afternoon Giles and George, the two bank managers and me, to discuss bundling together the existing Natwest overdraft along with the loan for Bezurrel, at Barclays in Truro. My sons and I were determined to drive our payments down. The Natwest had been taking 3% above base and if we were going to pull the accounts together at Barclays we wanted a lower rate. Also, I wanted to be sure they wouldn't ask for agricultural charges. David Vague said no, just charges over the properties. The land and property together were valued at nearly a million and the agricultural assets – livestock, crops and deadstock – not far off £200,000, at the time. We'd already filled in a Farmer's Balance sheet that showed all the details.

Charges over the properties were no surprise. But then they came up with a shock. They said we'd have to pay £250,000 for Bezurrel, not £200,000, because we had to buy the farm buildings. It was true that on the land we would take from Uncle Derrick, there were – quite close to the house – a number of old stone-built outbuildings, grain stores and so on, around a big well-drained farmyard, a Dutch barn and a modern lean-to cattle shed. If we wanted a better rate, that was the condition; we'd got to borrow more.

We would therefore need a longer-term loan than the ten years we'd been looking at. At the end of the afternoon, we came away satisfied. We'd borrowed £550,000 altogether for twenty years at half the rate we'd been paying before, plus we'd got a £100,000 secured overdraft. Vague thought – given his experience of local conditions and the weather – that the overdraft should be £125,000 but I told him that if we needed a temporary raise to the overdraft limit we'd come back to him. I said it might happen, because strawberries took time to establish and you couldn't review your outcome properly until the end of a three-year crop cycle. But I was optimistic, and expected a steadily improving result.

David Vague was quite delighted with us that day, and as we drove past a cottage for sale in Gwinear he said he'd happily offer George a loan to buy it with. George didn't accept. But in November 1992, we officially added the land and outbuildings at Bezurrel to our other six farms and got to work.

Making things happen

If we were going to convert Bezurrel land to produce strawberries by the spring of '93, we had a lot to do fast. George was still away in Worcestershire so it was up to Giles and me and the staff. The Eustice farms covered a much bigger area now, and mobile phones were just coming in, so I got one each for me and Giles and they saved a lot of time and trouble. Giles had learned quite a bit on his course and he suggested we got a bigger tractor. He found a big second-hand Case machine with four-wheel drive that would help us knock all the fields into shape. Bezurrel hadn't produced a crop in a couple of years because Derrick had effectively ceased to trade around 1990.

We had to buy a bed former, plus irrigation tape with a polythene layer above, to make beds for the new crop to go onto; and an irrigation pump to get water from a disused Bezurrel well. A local man advised us on the kind of pump we'd need. Different pumps give different flow rates and there are other considerations. We chose the right kind, but then a mining engineer came in and declared that he didn't think the Bezurrel well would yield enough water. We looked instead at a lake at Tregotha, a mile away, that I'd built for trout fishing. It was fed by streams, but if we started extracting from it, the streams wouldn't be able to replenish it fast enough unless we dug channels. We got a man with a digger in to do that. Then we had to build a pump-house to house the pump and its power supply, because it needed an expensive three-phase generator. We could have got three-phase from a mains supply that was no distance away, but the power line would need laying fifty yards across the corner of a neighbour's field, and when the electricity board asked permission from him, he wanted so much compensation that it was never going to happen.

The irrigation alone, for which we'd budgeted £25,000, what with one thing and another, was going to cost £45,000. Half-way through that traumatic spring, confronted by some further expense, I thought to myself: what can I do here? Should I give up? Pull out of this whole strawberry project and just carry on with vegetables? We were already so far down the line, into the season, keeping the bank informed – and they'd been warned it wouldn't be easy – I did waver, but I decided we'd invested so much time and work and thought into this - and strawberries, if they did well, made real money that vegetables rarely do. We drove on.

We did achieve some cost savings. We didn't need to build a new pack-house because there was quite a big shed at Bezurrel already which Uncle Derrick had used for cauliflower packing, and to park his lorry in. All it needed were a few amendments, tidying up and windows put in, plus sliding doors and tight insect-proofing, to make it good for soft fruit. One of our men did that. He also built a cold room for fruit storage. We'd bought an industrial chiller to go in it, with a heat extractor, but it needed a big electric cable from the yard about 150 metres away. Fortunately I already had enough of the right kind of cable, left over from the power line when we built the restaurant at Trevaskis.

By February of '93, after what had been a difficult winter, we'd got forty acres ploughed, ready to lay down and plant, all concentrated as far as possible near the pack house. Everything seemed to be going well. I'd taken on a couple of local men, one mainly as a tractor driver and the other, a farmer's son, as a general hand who could do just about anything. Between us we did a pretty good job of laying out the strawberry beds for irrigation and planting. We were all working seven days a week, weather and daylight permitting, because we were also having to harvest spring greens from Tregotha, and pack them and get them off to market along with the winter vegetables.

Later that month we would plant our strawberries. George, Giles and I had thought a lot about which varieties to plant. We'd visited three companies in different parts of England before choosing the type that would be best for us, at the fairest price, from R W Walpole up in Norfolk. Unfortunately they got severe frosts up there that year so they couldn't lift the plants when we wanted them and they arrived a few weeks late, so we couldn't get them into the ground until March. We had to find staff to plant them from wherever we could, at that point, and pay them piece work. Giles – at eighteen – was left to organise the hands we got and he made a very good job of it and enjoyed himself as well. One day the whole crowd of them decided to agitate. They huddled against the hedge and told him they weren't going to lift a finger until they got more money. He said 'You do that, then. I'll find other people to work for me.' They grumbled and went back to planting. He'd learned about farming at Trevaskis, and had dealt with the public in the farm shop and he'd been doing some of the buying for a while by then too.

We also planted five acres of Autumn Bliss raspberries. The idea was, that when the strawberries finished in July the raspberries would need picking, so we'd have an income late in the summer and something for the staff to do. We also rented tunnels from two other farms locally and raised Everbearer strawberries in pots and glasshouses. We'd plant them in the ground after the last frost, and then we'd have a supply in the autumn; a final burst of summer fruit. I was glad of that, because at Trevaskis and Tregotha, it hadn't been a good season for cauliflower and spring greens and we'd need a good summer income to make up for the poor winter crop.

At Bezurrel Uncle Derrick would wander over from the house to see what was going on. He was fascinated by all these new ways of doing things. Also, for the first time, he had the luxury of not having to worry about the outcome. He still looked after the British Lops for me, but he loved doing that.

March '93 was a busy month. Apart from everything else, at Easter, when he came home for the long weekend, George helped upgrade our accounting system. Until we got involved with Barclays the money had come in and out like the waves on the shore and had been recorded in a cashbook, and we'd relied on Kelsall Steele to make sense of it. However, David Vague and Trevor Furse were a lot stricter. George had got it all computerised and coded but he wasn't yet happy with the system we had. He was forever asking me about missing timesheets, asking why National Insurance contributions hadn't been recorded, and why I'd presented cheques a month after we'd got them. Also everything tended to go into one pot and it was not always straightforward to work out where the income from cattle ended and income from butchery began. I could see he was right. Our farms, with the addition of Bezurrel, were a much bigger business, but I didn't have time to keep the accounts up to date and, right now, nor did he. We desperately needed somebody until George graduated and came home. Rachel, one of Derrick's daughters who lived at Bezurrel, worked three days a week for a local auctioneer and she agreed to come in as our farm secretary on the other two days and do the books.

As spring came, we'd got twenty people planting out 80,000 potted strawberries in one week. Their wage packets were always made up at Trevaskis in the office and taken over to Bezurrel to hand out. Giles was making up the packets one Friday, along with Ron Rutter who helped us, when there was a knock on the door. A Lincolnshire fellow from the planting team was outside. He needed his wages early tonight, he said. They led him into the office and he snatched the whole bag of cash and ran out and jumped into a car where his friend sat waiting. As they shot away Giles and Ron tried to stop them – but had to jump for their lives.

Up the lane went the car, at speed. Adele was driving down. It's only about eight feet wide, that lane, and she saw a car that was clearly in a hurry so she didn't think twice; she reversed back to let them through. Giles, frantically chasing after them in his own car, didn't understand that instinct at all and shouted as he shot past

'What d'you do that for? They've just snatched all the wages!' He drove after them all the way down to Hayle, along the bypass. The driver in front swung a U-turn across the central reservation and so did he. He chased the two villains back to Hayle where they braked suddenly outside the butcher's shop, jumped out of their car and ran off. A minute later they were making their escape up the fields behind the street with Giles and Robin, the butcher, catching up on foot. When Giles grabbed the money back there was a fight, and the one who'd stolen it ended up with a broken arm, but the police arrived then and arrested both of them.

We got our wages back and the police got the thieves. Robin and Giles got their pictures in the paper. Also - another cause for happiness – the spring was warm and fine and the forty acres of strawberries got away nicely. That April, another neighbour said 'I hear your crops over Bezurrel are looking an absolute picture, Paul.'

I was pleased with that, because without friendly words of encouragement I'd have tended to focus on the weeds, which had put on a magnificent growth spurt at the same time as the strawberries, and needed hand-weeding, which, over forty acres, costs.

So in our first winter of big-time strawberry growing we'd had a whole series of obstacles and work-arounds and extended our overdraft but, in the end, we'd got it together. The crop looked very well, the pack house was up and running and we had everything in place to supply Kentish Garden. We started picking at the beginning of June and the early fruit was good.

On a hot day in the first few weeks of that month David Vague rang to ask if he could bring a visitor to Trevaskis.

'You know Trevor Furse is retiring. Well, you'll be dealing with John Bloor at Truro from next month and I'd like to bring him over.'

I don't think Bloor was used to being outside in hot sunshine. A thinnish fellow in his forties, he was in a white linen summer-weight suit but still perspiring heavily. I saw Adele flinch when she shook his hand because it was sweaty.

The two bank managers sat down for tea, and a meeting, in the restaurant. I explained the issues we'd had and how we'd dealt with them successfully. David seemed to see all these things as teething problems which we'd managed to iron out, and accepted that we'd been unlucky with a poor harvest of winter vegetables. John Bloor was tougher. He was concerned that we'd only just started and had already overrun our budget. He wanted us to put financial controls in place right away, because unless we had a clear idea of where we stood at any given moment we might overspend. I didn't have a problem with that. Then he said he wanted monthly cash flow reports, enterprise by enterprise, from us. We should have a full-time farm secretary who would deal with money coming in and out all day every day. Also, we needed to use Sage Accounts on the system because every other business did and it was immediately comprehensible.

I privately wondered how we were going to find time and money for what sounded like quite a major shake-up but willingly promised to improve our reporting. Right now, we'd been working long days, seven days a week, establishing a new business, and the paperwork would be taken in hand as soon as George came home from college at the end of the month. Bloor agreed to that.

When they left I told Adele

'That man's going to give us a lot of trouble.'

Sure enough, he put his requirements in a friendly but concerned letter, about how our accounting had in the past been opaque, and we were still exceeding our overdraft. I wasn't all that worried because they knew the reasons for the over-spend, and that we'd probably spend a bit more before the money rolled in. When George came home from college for good he was able to come up with a report which explained, in detail, exactly when and why we'd gone over budget. He sent with it a cash-flow analysis for the months from February until the end of May and a cash-flow forecast from July to October. We also told Bloor we'd be holding monthly budget meetings with Rachel, our farm secretary, and Alan Cook the herdsman.

-

In May, at Gwinear Field in Bezurrel, I had drilled two acres of winter cauliflower seeds. We would gather them as seedlings in four or five weeks, and plant them over 100 acres (optimally yielding 8,000 plants per acre, but even in a good year, closer to 6,000).

I used to do all the seed drilling when the days began to lengthen. One time, at dusk, I left the tractor and the drills ready to re-start the following morning, and set out to walk home. I took a short cut through Lanyon. When I passed the big house, Lanyon Manor, it was nearly dark, and suddenly I was cold. A horrible feeling of dread came over me.

Twice after that I tried to pass Lanyon Manor in the evening but I was overcome by that ominous sensation and had to turn back and make a much longer journey. There was nobody living in the house at the time. People had always talked of there being ghosts at Lanyon. It made me shiver. I could feel a presence there.

When we came to pull the cauliflower seedlings off that field late in June of '93 we had no luck at all. We'd only got to think of starting and there'd be torrential rain. So the plants stayed in the ground, and got bigger and bigger. By the time the weather was dry enough it was late July, and planting was difficult because what we were handling were already visibly cauliflowers and too big.

Once Bloor was in his new job at Truro, he came out to have a look at all the land we farmed. We had lunch in the restaurant and then I drove him around to show him exactly what we were doing, and of course that was a late-summer problem that I had to point out.

'I don't know how you can cope with it all,' he said.

'I've grown up with it,' I told him. 'It's been my life since a boy. It comes easy to me.'

He told me he wanted to see our overdraft back down below its £100,000 limit by the end of the summer, when winter vegetables were all planted and the autumn soft fruit was sold. I thought I'd like to see that, too.

-

That autumn was wet and miserable and the soft fruit didn't bring in anything like the amount we'd expected. We'd spent up to the limit of our overdraft after planting winter vegetables, which wouldn't show a return until mid-December. And all this, piled on top of the overspend on capital expenses last spring (the irrigation and so on) left us overborrowed to an uncomfortable degree, in spite of good returns on the summer fruit. Bloor was jumpy because I had sent cheques out before we got covering payments in and therefore, not only had we exceeded the overdraft limit, but he was more concerned than ever that our day to day accounting wasn't rigorous enough. He asked for a meeting to discuss a way forward. And as I well knew, our annual review was due next month.

Accordingly, in October, we went to Truro to see him. At his suggestion, we agreed that we'd like to add one hundred thousand of our existing debt onto the twenty year loan. Then we could start again, I thought, with an overdraft ceiling of £100,000 or probably £150,000 if we had bad winter weather. He wasn't averse to extending the loan at all; in fact he was sympathetic. He wrote to confirm what we'd spoken about, and promised that when he'd consulted people at the South West headquarters he'd let us know.

In November '93 he came to the restaurant to see me. The Bank was prepared to put £100,000 of our overdraft onto our capital loan, but only if it was repayable on demand. Barclays was also prepared to let our overdraft limit be £150,000 but on 31st July 1994 they'd take that back down to £100,000. Oh, and they wanted agricultural charges as security.

I felt as if I'd been hit by Mike Tyson. Bloor hadn't mentioned any such conditions at our earlier meeting. Our capital loan was repayable over twenty years. Those were the terms of the agreement we'd made this time last year. Not 'repayable on demand' and 'not subject to agricultural charges', either.

I didn't want to discuss this in detail until George was there, so Bloor left. When he'd gone my shock turned to anger. Farming has been volatile since the dawn of time and I thought bankers knew that. They were being wholly unreasonable. Our first strawberry crop had always been expected to be light, because that's the way with strawberries in their first year, as we'd explained in the Farm Plan and several times since; and considering that we'd planted late, we'd done very well. Farming is not a short-term gamble but a long-term investment. It has ups and downs. They were seeing only the downs, with a view no further than their noses.

I felt I'd been conned. I'd moved all my business over to Barclays and because of a series of circumstances nobody could have foreseen, we'd had a rocky start. Now they had me in their clutches they couldn't wait to squeeze me – which could finish us off just one year after we'd begun.

When George came back we brainstormed ways to clear the overdraft once and for all. I was overwhelmed by Barclays' unbearably intrusive, time-wasting and expensive management of our finances. I wanted them unconcerned with anything except the twenty-year loan we'd originally signed up for. We'd be back to regular automatic payments of known sums and they'd have no reason to pick over our accounts or pile charges upon charges.

I told Bernard Pooley, our accountant at Kelsall Steele, what my position was and how angry and betrayed I felt. I also told him that we could clear the overdraft with some big lump sums and I was willing to sell the house at Angarrack Hill Farm. That would bring the overdraft right down and the Bank would have no need for agricultural charges. Anthony, our tractor driver, agreed to vacate Angarrack Hill farmhouse if we could sell it.

Pooley came with me to a meeting at John Bloor's office in Truro. I told Bloor what I intended to do.

'Paul that's a rational move and it makes me happier. Good for you.'

He ran through the figures.

'The thing is, selling one farmhouse at Angarrack Hill won't really be enough. It will shrink the overdraft somewhat but the security available to the Bank will be lessened at the same time. I'm afraid we'll still want one year repayable on demand, and agricultural charges.'

'If I sign up to that,' I said angrily 'you'll be able to send Receivers in any time you want. I'll have no say in it and my business will be finished. Four generations of farming will be wiped out overnight.'

'I don't want you to see it like that, Paul. Believe me the Bank has no intention of doing any such thing. You know your farms and how to farm them better than anybody. These terms are a formality we have to put in place to protect our shareholders. And, of course, we have other local farmers banking with us and we wouldn't do ourselves any good if we made unreasonable demands on you. Everybody round here knows you're good at what you do.'

I was silent.

'Paul, before I came here I was in the City of London and I dealt with a great many Receiverships. I can assure you there's no way in the world that we want to take your farm. We would go out of our way to avoid that.'

I trusted that he meant it, but I still went home not knowing what to do. I had to service a big debt, but I couldn't whistle up money at will, while our animals needed feeding and our land needed fertilising, our crops needed harvesting and we all needed a roof over our heads. I had to be able to work, with confidence, with funds to invest in it all, so that we could make more money.

I just wished I'd never heard of Barclays Bank, where the people in charge didn't seem to understand that an enterprise like ours would sometimes have to demand leeway but would come good over time.

The whole thing went round and round in circles in my head; I felt trapped. I rang Bernard Pooley.

'Bernard, there must be a way out of this.'

'They've got you over a barrel' He said. 'There are not really other options if these are the terms they are setting down.'

With hindsight I think that advice was wrong. Another accountant might have said, well, your assets are valued at nearly £1.2 million, your capital loan will be about 55% of that, and your running overdraft will come down once this new enterprise settles. Another accountant might have made them see the point and got them to back off.

I had discussed with George a possible alternative. We could have put our foot down and refused to sign the agreement. We could have organised a cattle sale to realise working capital to maintain loan repayments. However, there would also be risks that the bank could retaliate by calling in the overdraft we already had which would then precipitate a technical default on the loan in any event. So there were risks to calling time on the bank at that stage too.

Bernard Pooley advised going along with their terms, subject to clear assurances from the bank that they were not lining us up for receivership. These assurances were subsequently offered by John Bloor and the bank. I didn't go looking for a second opinion from another accountant or another law firm. Who does? Maybe a financier would have been more aggressive than I was, but I had a farm to run.

My mother's loan to the business had been itemised in the accounts. Bloor wrote that he 'had not appreciated that the £50,000 introduced into the Partnership was intended to be a short-term loan rather than a permanent injection of capital...

payments to Mrs Eustice in the next 12 months should not exceed an amount equivalent to 5% of the capital sum presently owing to her.' That was just one damn thing. There were others. 'Interest on the loan is to be linked to LIBOR.' There were a lot of figures and fractions after that bit, and by then I knew what the London Interbank rate meant because he'd told me already, but there were contingent requests. 'To protect you from adverse interest rate movements, our minimum requirement is that you take out a three year CAP to cover half the loan.... The matrix enclosed with my letter of 6th November will...'

Oh my Lord. I knew we were having a run of bad luck and for the first time I was out of my financial depth. I just wanted Bloor to back off and let us trade through this as we'd always done before. His constant nagging made everything more difficult.

So, just a year after I started banking with Barclays, I signed the on-demand loan for £650,000, with the agricultural charges. And went home just when we were coming into our winter vegetable season which – and I don't know why but I wasn't surprised – would turn out to be a bad one. The winter of 93/94 in Cornwall was the wettest and windiest in a hundred years. It wasn't just the vegetable crop that suffered either. For many years we had grown anemones at Tregotha. Last summer we'd sourced some specially beautiful and hardy ones from Israel, and drilled them in over ten acres; we hired a contractor with a special drill to do it. When the weather worsened, we'd put up windbreaks every ten rows. Even so, the plants were flattened by rain and wind. As for the spring greens and cauliflowers, we'd planted 120 acres but we only made the profit we'd made off 80 acres the previous winter.

I began to feel leaden and dispirited and when I brooded I remembered bad things. For instance, an ignorant, sniping remark from last summer. A man who was on the Council of the Royal Cornwall Show with me had sneered that I'd never have been able to buy Bezurrel if I hadn't had family money behind me. I couldn't even begin to argue with him without telling him more about my affairs than I intended to. But when people imagine that 'family money' is available to a man because he inherited a family business, all is not necessarily what it seems. What I inherited was farmland and buildings and animals and debt, all of which needed expensive upkeep that had to be earned by the sweat of my brow. We had very little cash left over, ever, and at the end of a recession, when I bought Bezurrel, my existing land and houses were worth a lot less than they would be in a boom.

Adele and her sister Charmaine were our family's public face, always working their socks off, friendly and hospitable and serving good food to the visitors - and the shop and the restaurant were popular and profitable. But I've seen how people are jealous. 'All right for some,' they'll grumble. People who've never even dared try to run a business themselves. Around that time I had to make a conscious effort to ignore remarks like that because if I didn't, I'd become embittered. I had been patient and good-humoured before and I didn't want to turn curmudgeonly now. What Barclays Bank had really taken from me, for no good reason, was my sense of security. They were undermining my own self-worth.

In that blowy, sodden, cold winter of '93 -94 we decided to cover our strawberries in heavy polythene sheeting, weighted with sandbags, for protection and warmth. That way the crop would be ready early in the year when the price was high. We found an opportunity in February, '94 when the wind wasn't blowing a gale and the land wasn't sodden, and got on with it. George was supposed to run in the national championships up in Sunderland that weekend and his team were going up on the

Thursday, but he was too busy manhandling polythene to go. Instead I drove him up, through the night, on the Friday. He ran on the Saturday, did well, and we set off to drive back on the Saturday night. It was 460 miles; but when we finally drove by Bezurrel that windy Sunday, we saw great flapping sheets of torn polythene racked against the hedges and up in the trees. A bitter cold gale from the east had done that, yesterday and last night. When we got out there we couldn't even begin to shift that polythene back because the wind was still too strong, and the strawberries were nigh on wrecked.

I was overwhelmed with consternation and exhaustion. I thought of John Bloor, with his nine to five job, probably at this moment relaxing with the Sunday papers somewhere in the suburbs of Truro.

In the March of 1994 we found a buyer for the Angarrack Hill house at over £90,000. I looked forward to reducing the overdraft by almost that amount. A few months later the sale fell through.

Gale force winds and heavy rain persisted into May. That should have been pollination time for the strawberries, but they'd only managed to produce about 60% of the flowers they normally would. We knew the yield would go down by at least the same percentage, and so would our income from them, and up would go our overdraft, in the same measure.

Unknown to me, our situation was being played out politically within the bank's hierarchy. This became evident to me much later, when I saw the regular memos that flew back and forth according to the bank's internal procedures. Bruce Hammond the agricultural manager reported on our farms to John Bloor, the Truro Group manager; and John Bloor reported on our loans to Trevor Irons who was assistant risk manager in Bristol, almost 180 miles from us. Bloor was under pressure from Irons.

That May of 94, Hammond in his annual farm business appraisal recognised our difficulties but commented that in the circumstances, 'I think that the management has done remarkably well.' Our balance sheet showed assets of £1,165,000. He thought it was about twenty thousand less, but 'while the gearing of this business is undoubtedly high, I would consider the Bank's position safe with the security that we have which is a first charge on the land and property and an agricultural charge.' If even average strawberry prices were achieved this summer, 'then we should have no difficulty in continuing to support the business into the future.' Just one week later John Bloor, who had seen that report, sent Irons a cautious recommendation that we be allowed a short-term £200,000 overdraft, repayable on demand. This would be reviewed on 31st July.

Meanwhile we couldn't get labour. One weekend, we had acres of strawberries just about ready and good picking weather for once but we were so short of pickers that Giles and George even went door-knocking around the village offering extra money. They persuaded just one person to come over. We had to get New Age travellers onto our land to pick for us.

The good news half way through that summer was that, as George explained with his monthly cash flow report to Bloor, we were on course, but not in the way we'd expected to be. Essentially, we'd had poor soft fruit yields but everyone else's had been even worse, so in the scarcity we'd got paid more. And we'd managed our workers very carefully, and made cost savings.

This elicited the typed equivalent of a cold smile from Bloor. 'You need a better than budget performance if you are going to make up the ground you lost.... You ought now to be in a position to .... Could you please.... ' and so on. He was going on holiday so he wanted it all quickly. I felt like a galley slave.

Conflict brews

By the end of the summer we'd definitely sold Angarrack, and for a better price than we'd hoped. Sadly this meant that Anthony Mitchell, our tractor driver who'd worked with me since about 1970, had to leave his home there. We helped him find another cottage back in the village but we felt unhappy and disappointed about having to do that. And everything else seemed to be going wrong. We wanted to sell the outbuildings at Bezurrel with planning permission for holiday cottages. The planners gave a qualified yes, except that we had to widen the entrance to Bezurrel Lane from the road, for safety reasons. This meant bringing back each of its two corners by about three feet. One side was easy because we owned that land, but opposite one was a corner of somebody's garden. I visited the home-owner. He was a retired gentleman, recently widowed, and for some reason not keen on the idea although I offered all kinds of incentives, including more land as compensation.

However, he said he'd think about it. Having heard nothing after a few weeks I visited again. No, he said. His wife had liked that garden and he wasn't prepared to change it. His wife was no longer with us, but I couldn't change his mind. We had wasted time and money in an effort to get planning permission. I felt thwarted.

In August of 1994, with Barclays still grinding us down, George presented Bloor with a future plan, under the headings Problem, Strategy, Turnover, Management and Summary. We'd all discussed it, all five of us. I was never one to hide from uncomfortable realities. We had undertaken a major expansion to bring a large farm into our operation and we always knew there were risks in that. When the risk of unfavourable weather came home to hit us, we needed to react accordingly and we were certainly willing to.

George wrote a masterly document. He described our position much more tactfully than I could have done but still managed to convey that the bank had judged everything we were doing on the basis of one particularly bad year's results. They were panicking in what would always be a risk-prone business. Also, the burden of debt, plus the bank's insistence that we pay suppliers only at the last moment, was making success doubly difficult for us to achieve.

In his plan, George explained how we were prepared to recognise that fixed assets could be used to power future profits. We'd sold the Angarrack farmhouse and we would sell some cattle to raise another £40,000 and reduce the overdraft still further. We also intended to sell land at Angarrack, buildings at Bezurrel and Lemin farm. The whole bundle would raise £300,000. This would reduce our debt by around 35 percent, but without affecting the turnover or earnings potential of the business. It would restore the gearing ratio to normal levels without interfering with crop rotation and reducing the likelihood of healthy yields in future.

We proposed to concentrate our operations for efficiency. Storage and livestock would be at Tregotha, retail at Trevaskis, and our central pack house, fruit and vegetable fields at Bezurrel. Adele was willing to buy the farmhouse at Trevaskis and would almost certainly qualify for a mortgage since the restaurant was doing well.

We'd had ideas about maximising profit from other assets. George outlined further uses for the pack house, such as working with a tomato grower to raise early season soft fruit under glass, and renting polytunnels to grow winter flowers. There were plans even beyond these but George wisely kept the whole document short and punchy. Finally, he outlined an economical way to streamline the whole operation. We recognised that we had too few experts for such a big and varied farm, so he outlined a program for training key short-term staff fast - to do just one thing really well - so that they could teach and lead a team. Also, we'd have a financial controller in once a month to help Rachel and we'd make slight changes to the management structure.

The result was a pro-active business plan, bullet-pointed and supported by pages and pages of figures from the accountants. Given a breathing-space for debt reduction by selling the land and outbuildings as we proposed, we could succeed. However, we had to keep trading strongly in order to maintain goodwill, so this was absolutely not the time to start bouncing our cheques or hammering our overdraft into the ground.

We got a letter from John Bloor. He agreed that 'the information provided by you and by Kelsall Steele was well prepared and very helpful.'

Unknown to us, Trevor Irons, in Risk Management, was fretting after a phone conversation with Bloor half way through that August. Irons told Bloor that the overdraft *'causes us concern'*; the explanations for shortfalls *'do not provide us with any comfort'* and he demanded more information. Accordingly Bloor's congratulatory opening paragraph to us was followed with yet more queries about figures, all to be prepared within a couple of weeks (he'd got another holiday coming up).

Bruce Hammond visited in the first week of September. I showed him round and George and Giles explained exactly what we were doing. Hammond at least understood how weather-dependent our business was. We gave him the plan we'd given to John Bloor.

In his own report to Bloor he approved that plan and said the bank should stick with us because we knew what we were doing and had done a good job in extraordinarily trying circumstances not of our making. In the September '94 edition of *South West Farmer*, he even described our enterprise (unnamed) as a model for survival through difficult times:

"This is a business that had expanded rapidly and had a severe setback in the first year of expansion... After a period of consideration and planning there is now a new plan and strategy in which it is stated that 'we realise our business is no longer an asset-oriented business but must be a profit-oriented business. We now regard assets as a means to an end, rather than as an end in themselves.' If all farm businesses would analyse their situations in this way, define their objectives and plan accordingly, they would face future changes with much more confidence."

That article cheered me up and I read it over and over, although letters from Truro still seemed to arrive with every post. Our overdraft was to be £200,000, rising to £230,000 if it had to, but only for the next few weeks. I had noticed before that when Bloor allowed you to breathe for a minute, he always kept the gag in his hand ready to stuff down your throat. He had reported on G Eustice & Son to his Regional Office

'Their paper is well written and is evidence that they recognise the severity of the problems facing them and that they are prepared to take action.

Nonetheless, the measures that they propose would still leave the business with a borrowing requirement of £550/£600,000...'

This was an ill-judged lending that had been turned down by the Eustices' previous bank. Our enthusiasm was fuelled by the attraction of a large amount of new business for Camborne and the solution that the purchase by the Eustices of Bezurrel provided to a problem lending that Camborne had... There is no

101

doubt that weather conditions have played their part; all growers seem to have experienced the same problems with quality and yields this year .... The problem, as we have observed before and as the Eustices now recognise, is that the business cannot withstand the sort of setbacks that it has suffered this year.'

'The underlying strategy for both the bank and the Eustices must be one of controlled wind-down. In this context, I do not believe that the Eustices' proposals go far enough.'

He thought we should sell the South Devons, which, while not our most profitable enterprise, had an important role to play in good farm husbandry - offering crucial crop rotation and farmyard manure to go back onto the land that we were cropping. Basic realities of life and farming systems were alien to someone who had only ever known numbers.

'In the light of Bruce Hammond's finding we can determine what other expert opinion might be useful to us. We are likely to need recommendations as to the valuation and marketing of surplus property and we can quite readily call upon the services of either Lodge & Thomas or Stratton Creber.'

By this stage, it appears that there was a political split starting to emerge within Barclays. There were the agricultural experts in their agricultural advisory team who fully supported our plan, so much so that they cited it as a model approach for a business that had encountered a set back and responded with a clear plan to consolidate and get back on track. Then there were the bean counters in the debt recovery unit or risk management team who appeared to hold more sway but could not see past simplistic notions of "performance" from a narrow accountants perspective but with no understanding of the risks and uncertainties that were an inherent feature of agriculture. The risk management team seemed to find the advice of their own agricultural experts inconvenient. They were looking for something more aggressive.

The sale of Angarrack Hill farmhouse had given us £90,000 to take off our loan. We'd told the bank we would sell more land and buildings to the value of £300,000. Why wasn't that enough? Had we got above ourselves? I thought first maybe, then no, then yes, then no again, because paying down debt was on my mind all day, every day, and after a while the stress stops being cerebral and turns into a permanently heavy feeling in the gut.

That September I travelled the length of Britain, showing and judging cattle. I did a lot of committee work on shows and organisations, including the Royal Cornwall Show and our Gwinear Show, and I advised Gwinear and District Farmers; we were still doing considerable trade with them. For up to a week at a time my sons ran the farm and George, in particular, wrestled with the finances.

Up in Bristol, T J Irons was hatching his own ideas about the 'expert opinion' that could be sought next. Late in August, having seen Bloor's report of Hammond's recommendation to continue helping us, he'd insisted that '*If Bruce Hammond cannot be unequivocal in his support we should like him to nominate someone with the required expertise to carry out an assessment on our behalf.*' Irons wasn't getting the rigorous disapproval that he expected out of Hammond but was prepared to ask Hammond himself to get a second opinion – '*someone with the required expertise to carry out an assessment on our behalf.*' He wanted Bloor to '*give some thought to the necessity for a provision and therefore the submission of Form 207.*'

Form 207 signalled a gear change. Bruce Hammond had recommended sticking with us through another strawberry harvest in the spring and Bloor was minded to agree. He wrote to Irons at the end of September that he would '*prefer to defer submitting Form 207.*' In other words, let's not be too hasty here. Hammond had also suggested certain agricultural advisers, but his suggestions were ignored. Instead Trevor Irons responded approvingly to a sales pitch from Anderson's, agricultural consultants who operate all over Britain, and posted their glossy brochure to Bloor – who took the hint. The iron hand was about to slide out of its velvet glove.

Late in September Bloor wrote – unusually – a letter addressed to both myself and my mother. It effectively said that at this rate, we'd be working from hand to mouth forever, so he had arranged that Martin Redfearn, of Andersons Agricultural Consultants in Salisbury, would visit us soon. According to him, Andersons were coming in to help us with '*a more radical slimming down of the business designed to reduce borrowings to a level where the business is capable of sustaining itself.*' When Redfearn had seen what we were doing he might be able to contribute creative solutions to our cash flow problems, in case '*there may be something we're missing here.*'

He hadn't discussed with us, or apparently considered, any of the creative solutions we'd already put forward ourselves. Also, Anderson's charge, '*about £2,500*', wouldn't make our position any easier. We suspected that they would tell us nothing we didn't already know. But we had no choice. Andersons were coming anyway and what they would want from us was an up-to-date balance sheet, more of our time and more of our money. I left that, and our other work, to George, Giles and Rachel and the accountants and set off to Gloucester Market. Alan Cook drove one lorry and I'd brought a double decker down from Gloucestershire. Our 'radical slimming down' had begun already. We had to take about 40 head of our precious South Devons up there and sell them.

I fought hard to control anger and sadness. Alan Cook looked grim too. We'd had to let cattle go after my father's death and we'd only just got the herd back up to 120 cows and here I was, having to do this, to satisfy the bank.

We were herding them into the pens on the morning of the sale when my phone rang. Bloor was out of the office and this was his deputy on the line, pressing me for the £40,000-odd we were supposed to make.

'Give me a chance. The sale hasn't started yet. As soon as the money's in, you'll get it.'

They did, of course. Bruton Knowles conducted the sale and achieved the prices we hoped for. I would rather have kept my cattle but needs must. My daughter Serena gave me invaluable support by driving down from Shropshire, where she was now working. I will always remember and appreciate what she did that day.

In the first half of October 1994 Martin Redfearn and his colleague Richard Jackson, from Andersons, came to see what we were doing and to talk to us about our farming enterprise. They were far more interested in the value of everything we had than what we were doing with it. They immediately set about making a list of all they saw before them - which in itself set alarm bells ringing. I had understood from John Bloor that these people were agricultural consultants, so I'd expected them to analyse what we were doing on our farm and even come up with ways to achieve efficiency of a kind Bloor might understand. They seemed to know nothing. The practicalities of both winter vegetable and strawberry growing were quite new to them. They focussed on the figures and left us with a shiny brochure about their expert services. Their reputation as Agricultural Consultants, in contrast to their general bewilderment when confronted with the day to day business of farming, reminded me of something my friend Joe Lane had said in September, when we were driving around the country judging the herd competition.

'My old Dad always used to say, Paul, if you can get a name for early rising, you can stay in bed all day.'

I thought that fitted Redfearn and Jackson perfectly. In the ensuing weeks, in letters, they continued to demand more figures and sent a 'terms of reference' for my mother and I to sign. This situated G. Eustice & Son as their paying customer. I refused to sign it. John Bloor had agreed that I'd have to pay only half and Barclays would pick up the rest but as far as I was concerned Barclays had brought these people in so the bank was their customer.

By this time our attitudes had begun to harden. George in particular had started to challenge a lot of the assumptions and claims being made by these consultants. They later described him as 'particularly tenacious.' George had put forward his own quite radical plan that would have reduced debt by 35 percent. It is fair to say that I was reluctant to see assets go but was persuaded by George that we needed to meet the bank half way and recognise that things had not gone entirely as planned so a response was required. George felt annoyed that, having been so proactive in addressing the issue that concerned the bank, all they did was come back baying for more. Things might have turned out very differently if the bank had simply endorsed and worked with our own plan as their agricultural department advised. However, by this stage they were working to a different agenda set by their risk management unit.

I would have been hopping mad had I seen the initial briefing that Martin Redfearn had received. It came direct from Bloor's boss, T J Irons, the Assistant Risk Manager at Bristol. He had written to Redfearn and the whole tone of his instructions was – Give me an excuse to shut this one down.

But I had never heard of T J Irons and wouldn't get sight of that letter for nearly a year.

I was crossing Drannack Field on a tractor one afternoon, after sowing grass seeds, when I saw George walking from the house towards me, looking grim. I pulled up. He jumped onto the step beside me and said:

'Giles has just had Paul Cragg on the phone.' Paul was a Sussex grower we knew through Kentish Garden. He'd had trouble with the weather too.

'What about?'

'He's just had Andersons coming into his business too. They let their guard down and told him that they were doing some work for a bank on a big soft fruit business in Cornwall which has reached the end of the road.' Paul said that it was common practice for banks to put in putative receivers under the guise of 'consultants' in the first instance so that they could familiarise themselves with the business and its assets prior to the start of aggressive action.

The soft fruit industry has always been dominated by a handful of very large players who all know one another well. In that sense it is different to most sectors of farming. There was only one major player in the South West and that was us. A moment of loose-tongued candour by one of Anderson's advisers far away in Kent meant that the cat was now out the bag.

I switched off the engine.

'But we are nowhere near insolvency. The bank could not possibly send in receivers. They have promised us that Andersons are just here to help.'

Bloor had implied that Andersons might be the ones who could help our business innovate in order to grow. They might recommend a judicious pruning but not an immediate drench with glyphosate.

'Right.' There was a knot in my stomach. 'What do we do?'

'Paul has recommended that we speak to a specialist solicitor in Bristol who is the weapon of choice for most banks when dealing with conflict and receiverships but also has no qualms about acting against the banks. He also gave us a contact for an advisor called Des Phillips of Baybrook Securities.'

'What can he do?'

'No idea but Paul Cragg's advice is that we need to assemble a team to fight the bank and fast. He says that local accountants and solicitors cannot do this work effectively. It is a specialist task. You need battle hardened street fighters if you want to mount a defence against an institution that does debt recovery day in day out.'

That made sense to me. A lawyer. I tried not to worry about where the money would come from.

-

Des Phillips lived in a big house close to the motorway at Highbridge, west of Bristol. He was a lovely man with a Somerset burr, a farmer himself but he also had his own finance company. He said he knew what we were going through; he'd heard it from so many people, absolutely driven into the ground by the banks. I told him all we needed was time and we'd make the whole thing come good – but it looked as if Barclays was bringing in these people so that they could shove us over a cliff.

'Steady goes,' he said. 'There are things you can do. You need to hold them up as long as you can so you've got a chance to make it work.'

'That's right.'

Des got us an appointment with Peter Williams at Burges Salmon and, soon afterwards, on October 25th, we all went to

Narrow Quay House in Bristol to see Peter Williams and another solicitor, Dinah Close, at the firm's offices. Des gave them a very brief outline of our problem.

Peter Rhys Williams was a very clinical and precise solicitor. He was a wiry man in his thirties with red hair and a hearing aid he had had since childhood. He was proud to be Welsh but had no Welsh accent. You could tell that he was not the sort to do conveyancing, divorce or other run-of-the-mill legal work. He described himself as a "litigator", not a solicitor. He seemed to relish conflict, but to be fair to him, conflict with purpose. That is to say, conflict that leads to peace and settlement as soon as possible.

Peter Williams said:

'Let's get our situation clear before anything at all is said. You need to know that this firm has represented Barclays in the past and regularly. We've worked for them and against them, many times. You need to know that, because you may be concerned about some sort of conflict of interest. If it concerns you that we may work for the bank then now is the time to say.'

'We have no problem at all with that.' I said, 'We want someone who understands this area of law.'

'Good.' Replied Peter. 'As it happens I may have heard about your case already. I ran into the Barclays Regional Manager at the weekend at a rugby match and he said they might have some work for us on a case they have in Cornwall. The outline that he described to me sounds rather similar to your case. However, they haven't actually instructed us. If you choose to instruct me today then I would be conflicted out of being formally instructed by Barclays.'

'Once they realise that you have instructed me first, then they will probably go to their second choice law firm which is Bond Pearce at Plymouth. Specifically, they will probably instruct

Hamish Anderson who is a partner there. You need to be aware that both Bond Pearce and Burges Salmon, while independent, are part of the Norton Rose M5 Group which is a loose federation of westcountry law firms. We operate independently, but if you have a problem with that connection I need you to be aware of it.'

'It is not a problem for us if it is not for you.' I replied.

'To be honest, I have always found it more fun shafting your friends!' Peter Joked. 'However, on a serious note, there is wider context that you need to be aware of. Until recently Barclays Bank had a regional office in Plymouth and one in Bristol. Burges Salmon got most of the work around Bristol and Bond Pearce got most of the work in the far South West. However, Barclays recently closed their Plymouth HQ and, as a result, Bond Pearce have been getting very little Barclays work. If Barclays are forced to take their second choice option, then Bond Pearce may feel it is their chance to prove themselves again. While all solicitors have a duty to act responsibly and to seek to settle disputes, it is not clear how Bond Pearce would behave in this situation.

'So in view of this, I want you to consider whether we are the right solicitors for you. Would you like to discuss it with Des?'

'No. If you'll take us on we're happy.'

'OK' replied Peter.

'But there is just one other thing I need to make you aware of. If swords are drawn and this comes to blows and Barclays do decide to appoint a receiver, it is quite likely that the receiver they will choose will be Ryan Densham of Price Waterhouse. Ryan Densham is the brother to Andrew Densham who is a senior partner here at Burges Salmon and my managing partner. So I need you to be content that this does not create any concerns on your side.'

My word! This world of receivership was turning out to be quite incestuous! However, again I said 'It's not a problem for me, as long as it's not for you.'

Peter replied that none of this was a problem for him since he acted for and against the same people all the time and it was par for the course. He went on to say, 'It's unclear what Barclays would do. On the one hand, the fact that they have appointed Andersons suggests that something is going on. It has the hallmarks of a pre-receivership familiarisation phase. So they may appoint Andersons as receivers in the end. On the other hand, once they know Burges Salmon are involved they may decide to go for a more senior and experienced receiver and opt for Price Waterhouse. That's not necessarily a bad thing since a senior, more experienced receiver has the ability to influence the bank towards a more sensible course of action. An inexperienced receiver is more likely to just follow orders.'

Peter then asked if we had debt with any other banks or whether it was just Barclays. I replied that Barclays had required us to move all our business to them as a condition of advancing a loan.

'From my point of view that makes it simpler. A number of other leading High Street Banks pay Burges Salmon a permanent retainer in order to ensure that we can never act for their customers. Barclays is not one of those banks. They have expressed an interest in entering such a deal but they haven't yet. So we can act against them. However, if there were other lenders who got dragged in then our permanent retainer here at Burges Salmon would preclude us from taking up those elements of the case.'

'So some banks pay you not to act against them?'

'That is the practical and intended effect. In practice the permanent retainer fee is dressed up as payment to sit on an advisory board. However, it means that we are permanently conflicted out of acting against those banks who retain us in such a way.'

These revelations made me realise that we were right to be nervous about the way banks would behave. Why would a bank want to deny its customers access to legal advice?

Peter Williams then asked me to describe a little bit about the farms and the business and what issues we had been facing.

He and Mrs Close took notes as I told them the whole story, focusing on the hostile involvement of Andersons and the less than honest advice I'd had from the bank. Just about everything I thought would never happen, because Barclays Bank people had so vehemently reassured me, had in fact happened. I felt I'd been deliberately misled by John Bloor in particular.

'So your key grievance, if I understand you correctly, is that they reneged on your 20-year mortgage agreement.'

'Yes, they made it one year repayable on demand.'

'Did you expect that?'

'Never. I'd never have gone anywhere near them if I had.'

'We were having some set backs but John Bloor promised that they'd stick with us and would never send in receivers.'

'In writing?'

'I don't think so. But I took his word for it.'

Peter said 'verbal contracts are obviously always harder to establish but they are no less valid. It is fairly clear to me that you have a very strong moral case based on your description of events. The challenge is to establish a legal case.'

'One of the weaknesses of the law as it stands is that the remedy for a breach of contract along the lines you describe is only retrospective financial compensation. Therefore, a court would do nothing to stop a bank stripping you out, selling off all the farms and livestock. They will not issue an injunction on the basis of alleged breach of contract. If, after the event, it were found there had been a breach of contract then there would be financial compensation. However, by then it is too late because all of the farms and assets would be sold.

I looked at Des. 'Des was talking about possible use of tenancy agreements as a means of creating time and space.'

'Yes. Tenancies *can* be created which is then a legitimate ground to establish an injunction. Uniquely, agricultural property is treated differently by statute to other property assets. Under the Law of Property Act 1925, a landowner has a statutory right to create tenancies. While money-lenders always include clauses in their mortgage deed agreements that forbid such tenancies being created without prior consent, these clauses themselves are not valid since there is a statutory right in the 1925 Act that trumps it.

'However, there are some complications with such a course. There has been a test case recently – the Woodward case - where a new tenancy was set aside by the court partly because the rent was said to have created a ransom value over the bank. The judgement is considered by some to be rather shaky in legal terms but it is what the legal profession describe as a "public policy decision". That is to say, the courts have taken it upon themselves to create a precedent, which effectively establishes a particular policy interpretation of the 1925 Law of Property Act. However, we would need to consider how best to address this line of argument in order to avoid the precedent that had been created.'

This was an interesting discussion.

'We do have a long established tenancy on Tregotha.' I said, 'Granted by the partnership to me which was part of a tax management scheme.'

'When was that?'

'Oh, about 1980. Six years before he died.'

Peter had spotted an idea. 'One option might be if you were to assign this long established tenancy to the boys. That would make it much harder for the bank to resist.' He and Dinah Close noted down the potential for the Tregotha tenancy.

Peter then concluded by asking if we were really sure we wanted to press ahead.

'When swords are drawn and these conflicts start to unfold it can be very tough and distressing for all concerned. I need to be sure that you are robust enough to withstand the battlefield.

'We will do all we can and fight for your interests. Our duty, as is the duty of all solicitors, is to aim for resolution. The use of tenancy agreements is a perfectly lawful right established in statute. However, the heart of both your legal and moral case is that the bank acted in breach of contract by breaching an undertaking and withdrawing a loan agreement prematurely.

'They may seek to settle early and discuss things sensibly. It seems to me that all you require is space and time. One option that I might advise a bank to adopt in a scenario such as this would be to place all the debt on hold and facilitate an interest holiday for a limited period of time so that you have some breathing space to find an alternative bank and to refinance.

'It would probably be the most sensible and rational course of action open to the bank. However, they may act recklessly and choose to fight. Much will depend on the quality of the advice the bank receives from Bond Pearce and their appointed receiver and we will have no control over that. If they do fight then you need to be willing to see it through until they are willing to stop fighting and start talking.'

I was ready for the fight if that was what was necessary. Peter would later discover that we were perhaps more robust than he had actually wanted.

'We've got a family business here,' I said. 'We're not unstable, we know what we're doing, we've been farming that land for a hundred and fifty years and we mean to stay there. We're innovators, we're careful with our money, and we're three farmers, with three farms. In the long term the bank cannot lose. They're panicking over a hiccup. They've not had our account for two years yet. In farming that's the blink of an eye. We should do whatever it takes to keep trading.'

We left the meeting and set to work on constructing a legal mine field around our business in preparation for an imminent attack by the bank, should it come.

There was a scramble to get the papers drawn up and signed. The Andersons report was in the pipeline and, if it was negative, Barclays might jump on us. Redfearn and Jackson hadn't submitted it yet because my mother and I still hadn't signed their Terms of Reference. When we did, they sent it to us in draft form early in November. It was clearly aimed at Barclays Bank, not us. It was mostly gloomy and about money, although Redfearn and Jackson did venture to advise that we might have done better growing winter field beans instead of strawberries. 'Very clever,' I said when I read that. 'With the weather we've had in the past eighteen months, they'd have seen those beans flying past them at Salisbury.' Numerous other points were just wrong. In short, I thought the document was dismissive and in no way a recommendation to take the business forward. A cynical reader might see it as a pitch for a job as Receivers.

The Inland Revenue had been after us for a while and that same week, they issued a walking possession order. We had to sign it, or they'd confiscate equipment and machinery to the value of their claim. What it meant was that we could still use it all to earn a living, but the Inland Revenue had a first charge over it and could take it and sell it if we didn't pay them about £17,500 before the 10th of January. I didn't have £17,500 to hand, at the time.

Des Phillips had begun as a useful contact but was now acting as our consultant, although we weren't getting any bills from him. He came to Trevaskis on Friday 18th November for a document-signing session. Bob Seymour came over to witness to our signatures. I assigned the Partnership's existing Tregotha tenancy to the boys. We signed a newly created tenancy agreement to cover Trevaskis, Trenawin, Lemin, Angarrack Hill, Burnthouse and Bezurrel. The rentals had to be just a bit more than Barclays would get off me in mortgage interest payments, so that they could never claim they were financially disadvantaged by the tenancies. On the other hand, if the Receivers did get hold of the land while it was tenanted they'd certainly demand those high rates, which might bankrupt the boys. So payments – totalling £93,000 - were to be made six months in arrears and to be for three years. And we also signed a sale agreement whereby the boys bought all the livestock and deadstock, to be paid in arrears over ten years at a valuation yet to be made.

We informed traders that we'd changed our name and bank account. Bills and payments now went out on paper headed 'G & G Eustice.'

Adele was talking to Lloyds about moving her account away from Barclays.

Redfearn and Jackson listened to our objections and agreed to make some changes to their Report before they sent copies of the final version to us and to Barclays. I still thought it was harsh but I finally signed the Terms of Reference.

December 1994 began. I heard the postman struggling with the letterbox. At last a heavy envelope thumped onto the mat. Inside was a thick, expensively photographed promotional brochure, *Barclays in Agriculture*. Every article featured the bank's goodwill to all farmers and the wise advice they could offer us, and the whole thing ended up with a reassuring photograph of ten Barclays agricultural managers, including our friend Hammond, standing under a tree, grinning. I spied a corner of a country house hotel in the background. I thought they'd probably had a good lunch at their customers' expense.

On 8th December John Bloor called. He suggested a meeting to discuss Andersons' report and our way forward.

'Yes, I've seen it,' I said. 'I'm not happy with it and I want to discuss it with somebody at regional level as soon as possible. It looks to me as if Barclays Bank's lost confidence in my business. I don't know what's going on. I've been left dangling in empty space.'

'Well I'm still waiting for the October figures from Kelsall Steele.'

'You'll be waiting until we have the money to pay them to do the work. We already owe them six thousand because you keep asking for all this paperwork.'

'You're being rather confrontational Paul – '

'No I'm not confrontational. But I've engaged Burges Salmon and I intend to take legal advice before I talk to the bank again. In the meantime your head office can talk to my lawyer.'

There was a pause. 'I'll have a word with Regional,' he said. 'If there's a problem I'll call you back.'

The following morning, 9th December, a letter arrived from Truro, saying the bank would not pay our cheques.

Another letter, copies of which came by courier to myself and my mother that afternoon, was from Barclays registered office in the City of London. It was a formal demand for a sum of £758,476.05.

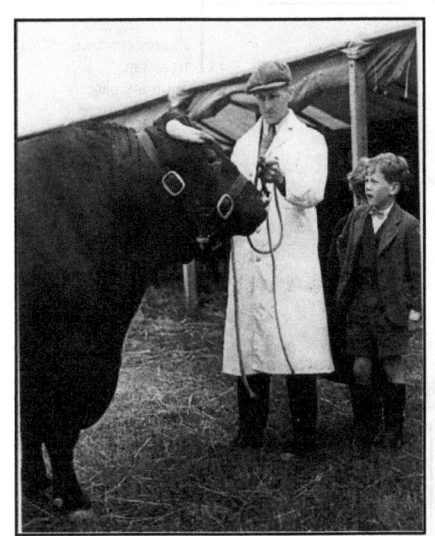

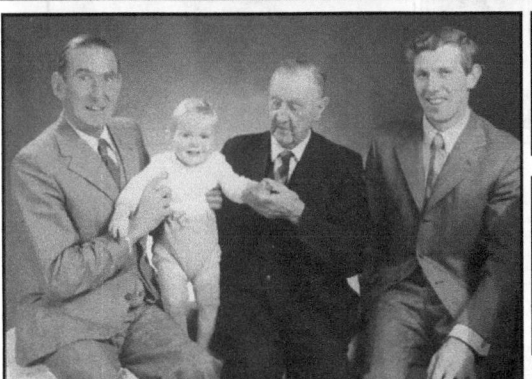

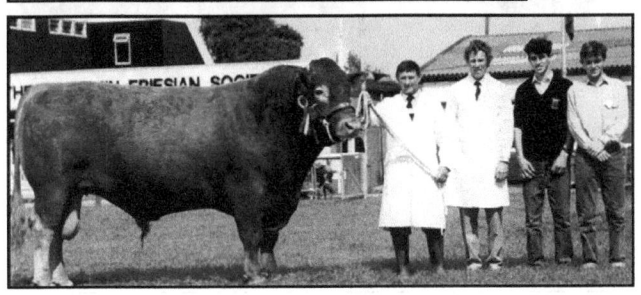

Photos clockwise from top left: Me as a boy; with Harry Wright; The Farm Shop in the 1980s; my Great Great Grandfather (left) with his son and grandsons at Bezurrel in the 1880s; my father at a show; with the boys & Alan Cook at The Royal Show 1992; Four Generations of George Eustice.

119

Photos clockwise from top: With my parents Inez & George and sisters Catherine & Mary in the 1950s; my three children, Serena, Giles and George 2015; on my wedding day at Lands End 1967; with Catherine & Mary in later years.

120

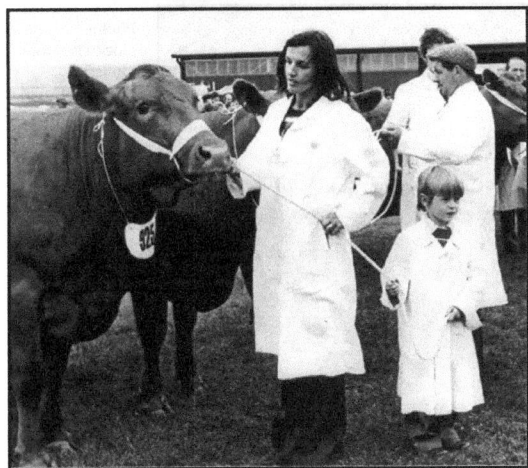

Photos clockwise from top: With my father and Grandfather in 1960s; With my cousins in 1950s; Adele with our son George at The Royal Cornwall Show in 1977; my three children, Serena, George & Giles late 1970s.

121

Photos clockwise from top left: Showing David Cameron around Trevaskis Farm in 2008; the farm shop in the mid '80s; The Queen Mother meets Alan Cook and one of our Bulls; me and the family on George's 21st and Giles's 18th birthday; on a family day out in Norfolk in the early '80s.

122

The descent to hell begins

Peter Williams, at Burges Salmon, sought a meeting, which he would attend, between me and Trevor Irons. We wanted to have a sensible discussion about a way forward. Our primary aim was to be given the space to refinance with another bank as we had discussed with Peter at our initial meeting. We had considerable assets, were nowhere close to being insolvent and our own plan for consolidation had been approved by Barclays Agriculture just a few months earlier. We could give them their money back but we just needed time and space.

However, as Peter Williams had predicted, Barclays had appointed Hamish Anderson of Bond Pearce, based in Plymouth, to represent them. Internal memos disclosed later in the trial revealed the senior management of Barclays Bank discussing how "much depends on a duel between the solicitors." Whether Bond Pearce advised a hostile course of action because it suited their interests to get one over Burges Salmon or whether the bank had already resolved on such a course remains unclear. However, the bank refused to meet or discuss anything.

The bank formally 'crystallised' the floating charges over our livestock and crops, which meant that that these were now fixed charges which could be claimed at will. They had already appointed an LPA Receiver, a man called Grant Watson who worked for Alder King, surveyors, in Exeter. A Land and Property Act Receiver can sell a debtor's property and collect rent on behalf of the bank. At about 5pm on Friday December 16th, a man from Alder King's Truro office marched into the restaurant and tried to present Adele with a document on Watson's behalf.

There are only two interesting things to say about this fellow from Truro, a relation by marriage whose name was Richardson. One is that both his wife and I ran for Cornwall at the national Championships in 1962. The other is that he was an idiot, because he hadn't bothered to investigate the extent of the property in question. The restaurant wasn't ours.

'I want you off the premises,' Adele told him. 'This is a separate business and has nothing to do with G Eustice & Son or Barclays Bank. Get out now, please.'

He stomped out into the cold and dark and tracked me down from there. I took the paperwork and said nothing. In the morning I called Peter Williams. He immediately applied for an injunction to restrain the Bank from sending the LPA Receiver in to sell the farms, on grounds that we would appeal, and the business was viable and needed time in which to trade. Barclays were now aware that we no longer held our assets, and counterclaimed that my sons' tenancies were a deliberate attempt to defraud the bank of what they considered their security. Judge Raymond Jack, at Bristol High Court, ignored that and found in our favour. The bank's men then decided to try to go behind the back of the Judge who had heard the case and try a different one. Two days later, on 22nd, Judge Jacob reversed Judge Jack's judgement at the Court of Appeal and directed that the case receive a full hearing in Bristol.

On Friday 23rd December Martin Redfearn turned up at the farm, as the stand-in for Mike Greetham, the senior partner in Andersons who was one of their two Agricultural Charges Receivers. He'd come to pick up the receipts from the Farm Shop, which had to go into a Fixed Charge Receiving Account, apparently, pending ultimate resolution of the dispute. I told him the receipts were not mine to give to him. George and Giles were the tenants of the Farm Shop and proprietors of the business.

'Since when?'

'Some time ago now.'

Our lorry, visibly loaded with vegetables under a tarpaulin, was parked at the top of the lane. I had to drive it up to Lincolnshire that night.

'Where are those cauliflowers going?'

'Up north. The Midlands and Lincolnshire.'

'Who'd you sell 'em to?'

'That's my business.'

Sigh. 'All right Paul. I'll be back in the morning.'

'I won't be here.'

'I'll talk to George.'

I drove north that night with John Benney. We always took it in turns to drive. On the way back we stopped at a service station festooned with ads for the National Lottery. It had only been going about a month then. We'd had a few other preoccupations at the time, but on Saturday nights on the telly, about twenty million people watched Mystic Meg, a crone in purple satin and a jet black wig, waving her long fingers above a crystal ball amid a cloud of dry ice and predicting what might happen. Every week some lucky person won about £5 million. Tonight's would be the first Christmas Eve draw and John bought a ticket at the service station. With odds of 14 million to one, I didn't hold my breath. (Or buy a ticket.)

The following morning – Christmas Eve, a Saturday – Redfearn turned up at 9.30. Like Richardson, he made the mistake of walking into the restaurant only to be turfed out by my wife. As he turned to go George walked in and presented him with two envelopes, one from Giles and one from himself. These enclosed signed statements to the effect that Charles George Eustice and Giles Paul Eustice were tenants of the farms that G Eustice &

Son had held before, and legitimate holders of the equipment, the livestock, the crops in the ground and the farm shop. The bank therefore had no right over any of it or any money received by the shop. As it happened the Inland Revenue had a prior claim to our farm equipment, and if we didn't pay them they could choose to confiscate it in January, and Barclays knew that. But our aim remained – to play for time. As long as we could stay in business until our income rose in the spring and early summer, we'd get over this. The law would grind on in the background but we had to continue as though we intended to survive.

We had a week of peace between Christmas and New Year. No sooner were we into 1995 than a writ arrived. My mother and I, plus George and Giles as tenants, were being sued by Barclays.

At another hearing early in January both sides undertook not to sell or dispose of capital assets pending a full High Court trial. In the meantime Andersons would oversee our operation.

Redfearn turned up alone on 9th January. He walked all the farms that day, compiling an inventory of machinery, livestock, crops and so on with George. He was reserved but friendly enough. There were no fireworks.

I had to discuss all these developments with my mother at Tregotha. She was in her late seventies and the worry was bad enough for us. What it would do to an old lady I didn't like to think. When we did talk about it, she agreed that we would go ahead and fight any court case on her behalf.

-

There was a good deal of to-ing and fro-ing in these early months of '95 between Bond Pearce and Trott and Battell and Peter Williams. Barclays behind the scenes had been alerted to the fact that the Partnership's original tenancy of Tregotha (dated April 1979) had in fact run out of time six months before we transferred it to George and Giles. It had never occurred to me that the original Tregotha tenancy came up for renewal after fifteen years, because for all of us it had been nothing more than a formality in the first place. But it didn't matter because the Partnership had continued to hold it, with the permission of the freeholder (me).

At trial, we would assert that Barclays had breached their November 1992 contract, which said they would support us over 20 years and that the express condition of our allowing the loan to become repayable on demand was a solid undertaking that the bank would not proceed to receivership.

Barclays' defence would say that our difficulties had been worse than they were entitled to expect and there never was any undertaking, implicit or declared, to support us over 20 years if their money was at risk.

Barclays would also counter-claim that the tenancies granted in November '94 were aimed to undermine their security; In our counter-claim we would make clear that we had a statutory right to create tenancies, that the payments under the tenancies meant there was no impact on the bank's security and that all we sought was time for our new venture to come good.

Where this left any of us was up to the lawyers to decide.

Martin Redfearn turned up at Trevaskis with Richard Jackson and Mike Greetham, his senior partner,(the Receiver for agricultural charges) on Friday 13th January, 1995. He introduced Greetham and then had to leave. He had to speak at some farming function up in Newquay.

'Will you tell them what you were doing down here?' I asked, as I took him back to the door.

'No.'

'Good thing for you then, because you might not get out alive if you did.'

I went back to the kitchen, where Greetham, Jackson and George were discussing the facts and figures we'd got to provide. On Des Phillips' advice we were recording all meetings with the Bank or its advisors, and a hidden tape recorder was picking up everything they said.

Andersons were going to take over our farm, apparently, and run it for us until the High Court trial. The implication, as I heard it, was that they'd be more efficient and therefore more successful than we'd been, and thereby prove to the Judge that our problems were of our own making. I could hardly keep the grin off my face. I was quite excited, as I was pretty sure that Redfearn and Jackson couldn't run a bath.

And by the end of the month it was becoming all too obvious that the two experts who were theoretically managing the farm were not even at the end of a phone line. They were employing us (Giles and George and I were getting £250 a week each – we'd never had so much cash) and we were doing whatever they told us to; but they were working five days a week from Salisbury. So when, on a Saturday or Sunday, the abattoir wanted a decision or a supplier needed an order number or the vet prescribed medication for a sick cow, they were unavailable and we had to go ahead, whatever it cost, to satisfy an impatient supplier or to save the cow's life. Where before we could have picked up a phone and ordered more rabbit fencing, new secateurs, ear tags, or polythene sheeting – now we had to send faxes to Salisbury first, and we rarely got an answer on our first attempt. We did our best to collaborate with Martin and get him to understand that big mixed farms work 24/7 all year round, and don't hold permanent stocks of everything they might need to supply or replace; but to some extent these difficulties remained. And administration took far too much of George's time, because he was duty bound to supply detailed daily incomings and outgoings to Greetham.

In the last months of 1994, and the first weeks of the New Year, we'd been slow to pay bills. Once the Receivers were in, our creditors got their current bills paid, although we remained in debt for outstanding amounts from before they took over. Most of our suppliers stuck by us because I promised that as soon as we got through this, we'd pay them. One whose good will I particularly appreciated was Joanne Richards whose business was the abattoir. She was already a creditor, but she continued to deal with our livestock and meat deliveries as she always had, supplying pork and beef to the Farm Shop butchery and the restaurant. I also owed money to the haulier who used to take the animals over to her, but when he heard about the Receivers he wouldn't take any more work from us, paid for or not. We found someone else quite easily; Neil Vincent, who lived at Helston, said yes as soon as I asked and proved to be a good friend.

There's a local firm of auctioneers, run by Richard Eddy and John May. John in particular we'd known for years. One day he was in the restaurant when it was empty. We talked about how the boys were tenants now. I noticed that he was suspiciously well-informed, and more reserved than usual.

'Ninety-three thousand in rent, I heard. What're the boys going to do, then?' he sneered. 'Go up to Angarrack and have a whip-round for it?' Angarrack is a tiny village. I didn't like his tone one bit, and later on I remembered what he'd said.

When people suddenly found themselves being asked to trade with G & G Eustice instead of G Eustice & Son they were bewildered and often suspicious, as you'd expect. I needed to explain our situation to many people we'd done business with for years. Gwinear Farmers let me down, I felt. I owed them £10,000 but I was still on their Committee and I didn't feel that I should be, in these circumstances. So I went down to the Chairman's place one weekend to talk to him. I was completely open about our difficulties and explained that we were working hard, but needed time to recover from unexpected setbacks. We'd be able to trade normally again once we were back in profit and had sorted out our situation with the bank.

'The thing is,' I said 'I know you're getting paid now, because the Receivers are in. But I haven't forgotten the £10,000. I don't feel good about it, so I don't think it's right for me to be at your meetings.'

'You should come down and tell all this to the Committee,' he said.

'No, I don't belong there at the moment. I'm telling you so that you can pass it on.'

I'd faithfully given them a great deal of business over the years, rarely questioning their prices on small items, and was likely to do so again. In order to support a co-operative that my grandfather had helped establish. For the next year, Gwinear Farmers were paid by the Receivers. They didn't chase me for money outstanding on my account. They said nothing. It would be a year before I discussed it with them again.

My cousin Martin at Hay Farm in Wadebridge was a great support to me. We talked often, he consoled me with advice and help, and he knew what he was talking about. His father, my Uncle John, had died now but Martin was still farming and he knew people who'd gone through exactly what was happening to us.

Our neighbour Robert Marks at Higher Trevaskis was sympathetic. After last winter's storms he was thanking his stars that he'd retrenched the year before. He'd let his farmland and his pack house to Piccavers, the big Lincolnshire company. He still lived in the farmhouse and had properties in Camborne, but he'd chosen to be a landlord rather than persist here because his potatoes and winter vegetables had suffered so badly in our recent bad weather. The main difference between him and me was that a few years before, he and his brother had sold some land to a developer and made a tidy profit.

Robert Marks had something to fall back on. If I'd rented out our farms to strangers I wouldn't have got enough rent to pay the bank; and since the only job I could do was farm, I couldn't have brought in a significant income to top it up.

Also, I had the misfortune to set a lot of store by tradition. I believed we belonged on this land. I still do believe that. If we lost it, I would feel that Uncle Derrick had handed his lifelong achievement on to me, and I'd let him down and besmirched the Eustice family name. No amount of reasoned argument from my family could erase that distress.

In mid-January '95 Barclays had appointed John Richardson, from Alder King, to act as Law of Property Act Receiver (LPA receiver) to market our entire holding of land and buildings. Under the law that applies to agricultural businesses it is normal to have two separate receivers. Andersons were appointed at the Agricultural receivers under the 1928 Agricultural Credits Act to manage the farm assets like stock and crops, while Alder King were appointed under the 1925 Law of Property Act to manage the property.

In most other business sectors, old style receivership became discredited and was replaced by "administration" under the Insolvency Act, and later the Enterprise Act, in the 1980s and early 2000s. However, the modernisation of the law slightly passed farming by and old-style, sometimes abusive, receivership arrangements remain the norm to this day.

John Richardson came to walk the farms with a view to putting them on the market as an agricultural investment, with George and Giles as sitting tenants.

One night soon afterwards, when we were all talking about ways to raise funds and hold onto our farming business, Rudi Mock rang me. He was a former prisoner of war, a German national originally, who had stayed on here and married a Land Army girl. Eventually, thanks to imagination and hard work, he'd become wealthy from his own big daffodil-growing business. He even got an MBE. He still lived in Praze.

'I would like to talk, Paul. I think I have an idea that might work for you. Could we meet, maybe?'

'Certainly. Come over now if you like.'

He did. He commiserated about my difficulties. He'd heard something of them; everybody had. I told him how the bank had deceived us; told us they'd support us through the first few difficult years of the strawberry project, gave us a twenty year loan and then pulled the rug from under us. He nodded sympathetically.

'I might be able to help. I have some friends in Jersey, Jersey Growers. They grow daffodils, and they've been looking at a farm on the Roseland here.'

'Oh yes?'

'Yes. I took them over there. But when I saw it,' he said 'I said, that'll be no good. You're too far east and they'll get chilly over there. They don't flower in cold soil.'

I didn't have to be a genius to see which way this was going, and I didn't like it.

'I said, I think I might know a better place. Paul, your land would be right for daffodils. And the way the banks are – it's a hard life. None of us is getting any younger.'

I was disappointed. I had hoped for – I don't know what I'd hoped, but I didn't want to hear this.

'I'm not selling up.'

'Think about it. You'd be better off out of farming. It's big business these days. If you do decide to sell my friends would offer a good price.'

'I know this is difficult. Change is always difficult. But if the bank is going to take your land it's best for you to control the sale. Sell it to people who want it.'

Rudi had not realised the reality of our situation. The banks had already appointed LPA receivers so were not in a position to hold any discussions of this sort. In any event, I wanted to retain our farms.

'The bank isn't going to take my land.' I wanted him to go away. I didn't want to continue this conversation. 'My sons are both farmers. We are going to keep our farms intact. We are fighting the bank.'

I think he sensed my agitation, because he left soon afterwards and I could hardly wait to see him out the door. I suppose he meant well. And later on he sold his own big business to those people from Jersey. But never in a million years would I offer my farms for sale.

At Alder King in Truro, John Richardson had been awarded an interesting job. He rubbed his hands and got on with it. Part of Barclays' case against us was that by creating the tenancies, we had diluted the value of the security we had given them – farms with sitting tenants being worth less than farms without them. When we came to court we would argue that the rent payable by George and Giles was so high that the price achievable by the farms remained the same.

Richardson was charged with proving it, one way or another (bearing in mind, of course, that Barclays was his client). In January, he walked the farms; in February, a glossy prospectus was ready. National and local newspapers and magazines would carry advertisements for 'the holding', that is, Trevaskis and Tregotha land with their farmhouses and outbuildings; and land and buildings at Trenawin, Angarrack Hill, Burnthouse, Lemin and Bezurrel. All but Tregotha were tenanted. Tregotha, according to the particulars, seemed to be tenanted on an expired lease, and Alan Cook was a sitting tenant of his cottage because he'd lived there 28 years.

Richardson had to come up with a method of sale and a price. He decided to offer the whole lot together, by private treaty between buyer and seller, and not to advertise the price largely because he wanted interested parties to make an offer. A lot depended on whether they personally saw the big strawberry enterprise – which came along with expensive associated arrangements for irrigation, chilling, packing and so on – as a bonus, or a dead loss. He had to have a figure in mind, though, so he decided that the minimum acceptable was £750,000. He based that on an estimate (in my view, an under-estimate) of what might be achieved with vacant possession.

He placed advertisements everywhere, from the *Observer* to the *West Briton,* for nine consecutive weeks from mid-February, and did his best to sort genuine queries from time-wasters. Most wanted vacant possession, but 59 were 'investors' and therefore potentially interested even with tenants in place. Until they heard the price, which was a vacant-possession price.

I didn't know this. But then, I was quite downcast enough, already.

In the middle of March John Richardson was interviewed by a woman from *Farmers Weekly* about our land, and for reasons known only to himself he told her what the reserve price was and that the land was nearly all tenanted. Enquiries slowed to a trickle after that, and he cancelled further advertising after March. Out of 155 respondents, just four remained. Three would drift away, leaving only Jersey Growers, who could buy land here a lot cheaper than they could in Jersey. He arranged a visit for them.

The Cornish Bloodbath

Adele's birthday is on 4th April, and in 1995 it began in the most harrowing way possible. We'd both been up half the night with my old dog, Sam, because he was very ill and in distress. We were very upset but we could see that he had suffered enough. I stayed in with him and called the vet out.

At ten to eight, Adele set off to open up the restaurant as usual. Since before Christmas she'd had a big notice up: BARCLAYS CHEQUES NOT TAKEN HERE. Maybe that gave some people the idea that she'd have cash in the place. She didn't. The till drawers were left open and empty, overnight. She never kept cash there. But when she got there on 4th April, she was horrified. The restaurant had two sets of double doors with glass panels. The glass had been smashed and the doors levered off with a big pole that lay discarded on the ground. Both sets of doors had been hurled across the restaurant leaving long splintered pieces of wood and shards of glass all over the floor.

Charmaine arrived. The two of them swept and tidied as best they could and Charmaine opened for business while Adele came back to the house and called out a carpenter and a locksmith. They'd fix it up that day.

Shortly afterwards the postman knocked at the farmhouse door for a signature. Inside the envelope he delivered was a formal notice that Barclays would shortly be going to the High Court to try to get our injunction lifted so that they could send Watson and Greetham in as LPA Receivers with full powers.

At nine o'clock John Richardson turned up driving a mini-bus full of Jersey Growers. They would be walking the farms. Adele went out to them.

'We'll keep out of everybody's way as much as possible,' he said, cheerfully. 'We'll probably take most of the morning so d'you think you could book us all in for lunch at your restaurant? Six of us – about twelve thirty?'

He always looked immensely pleased with himself, that man; even the sight of him made me grit my teeth, he was so tactless. Adele was completely calm and professional and took his order. Back at the restaurant, she made sure that the carpenter worked behind a screen and all the customers were served as usual.

I already knew who the Jersey Growers were and what they wanted. Adele and I had been friendly for years with a Truro couple, Dr David Gould and his wife Jane. Jane ran an outside catering business called Truly Scrumptious. Her company had laid on an afternoon tea hosted by Barclays Bank. The guests were Jersey Growers. Jane wouldn't have known who they were, if they hadn't talked freely about buying our farm in her presence, and I wouldn't have known if she hadn't rung up and told us that Barclays was already pulling out all the stops to attract buyers.

Mark Vandervliet, of Jersey Growers, had told Richardson that they'd only be interested in buying our land if it came with vacant possession. They would then offer a carefully worded tenancy, or even purchase of a part, to Giles and George. That would suit them because their daffodil operation required rotation, and would use a different 25% of the land with each successive planting, leaving the rest; G & G Eustice would be able to pick up the slack. In the end nothing came of it.

John Richardson's report was designed to give Barclays Bank the ammunition they wanted for trial. 'The reaction of the market place was as though the leases were a sham... (respondents said) the passing rent for the main holding was extraordinary and would be reduced at an arbitration at the first opportunity.'

On 20th April, Barclays Bank and their LPA receivers from Alder King, appealed to the High Court against the injunction that had so far prevented them from selling our property. They failed to get permission to proceed. Judge Jack decided that there must be a full court hearing, in Bristol, to decide the case once and for all.

In order to find out, Discovery must take place within the next month or so. In Discovery, each side would transparently, and honestly, disclose to the other their own record (letters, invoices, legal documents, notes and so on) of what had taken place leading up to Barclays' attempt to send in Receivers. When the case came to court, lawyers on both sides would be armed with information on which to base cross-examination. However, it is an established principle of justice that communications between defendants and plaintiffs and their respective legal advisers is privileged and should not be disclosed to the court. In the normal course of proceedings any information leading up to the point of an action being taken is made available to the court. However, in order to safeguard the integrity of the legal process, it is essential that those caught up in legal proceedings can have frank advice and it undermines due legal process if this is disclosed.

However, the bank sought to overturn this important feature of law by arguing that there was a prima facie case that we had shown sharp practice by introducing tenancy agreements, that we had sought to defend ourselves against a legal action by the bank and they argued that the law should favour money lenders over farmers in this instance and that the veil of legal privilege should therefore be lifted. They argued, to be specific, that there was a "prima facie" case that we had sought to defraud the bank. It was an extraordinary claim that held no credibility but it was, surprisingly, upheld by Judge Jack who heard the case originally.

We had discussed with Peter how to deal with this challenge. Peter was very relaxed regarding the substance of the material that might be disclosed. It said nothing remotely new. All the relevant information about the tenancies and the reasons we had created them had already been volunteered in affidavits for earlier hearings at the beginning of the conflict.

There was also actually nothing whatsoever to support the bank's contention that we had acted with any impropriety. On the contrary, as the Trial Judge was later to observe, we had simply acted to protect our commercial interests and we did so after seeking legal advice from solicitors of the highest repute. The fact remained that the statutory right to create tenancies on farmland took precedence over clauses in a mere mortgage deed. Peter had even mooted the idea that we might defend ourselves against the challenge from the bank and then disclose the information anyway since there was nothing in any of our dealings that anyone should feel ashamed of in a free society under the rule of law. However, we did believe that the judgement should be challenged since it was wrong in law.

The High Court Judges who presided over the case had no interest in hearing evidence from people who actually understood what had gone on and could have enlightened them as to the legitimacy of the action we took. As usual, it would just be a technical and detached argument among barristers. Lord Justice Schiemann, Dame Elizabeth Butler-Sloss and Lord Justice Aldous came down in favour of the bank again in what became a highly controversial test case. The disclosure of the information was of no use to the bank since there was nothing new.

Judge Weeks, who took the main trial some months later and, uniquely among the judges involved, took evidence from me and the rest of the family was rather scathing of the High Court Judgement. He described it in his own trial Judgement as "extraordinary". He also found that both I, and my family, had acted honestly and honourably throughout.

Other serious people in the law profession were also alarmed by what they regarded as something of a rogue decision. Peter Williams had been in discussion with the Law Society who had provisionally offered to sponsor a challenge to the decision in the House of Lords. Their concern was that the judgement could be abused by others seeking, for instance, to set aside legal privilege regarding perfectly legitimate tax avoidance strategies. However, we took a tactical decision to place such counter attacks on hold until after the trial. The bank's legal advisers knew that they had got lucky, that the Court of Appeal Judgement was not safe and was likely to be reversed in the Lords. That added to our negotiating position.

Cracks appear in the bank's position

Back at the farm, a different sort of problem was brewing. By late April there appeared to be the first signs of tension between Barclays Bank and Andersons, their chosen receivers.

Andersons had been required by court order to run the business forward which meant that order numbers were given for all manner of expenditure in order to prepare for the forthcoming strawberry crop. It meant that the day-to-day management decisions were, technically, made by the receivers remotely by agreeing order numbers but, in practice, they relied heavily on us doing all the actual work.

Mike Greetham from Andersons was now in a panic and running around like a headless chicken. His firm had agreed expenditure of over fifty thousand pounds but he was now worried that the bank would not honour that spending and would leave him high and dry.

In a tense meeting where he looked disturbed and animated, he complained that the bank might do him over, hang him out to dry and refuse to reimburse him for the money he had spent.

They might, he said, simply tell Andersons "tough luck, this is commercial risk." A part of me wanted to tell him, "join the club" but I refrained. However, he was clearly highly stressed. As he sat at the table in the restaurant, his legs were bouncing nervously. His message was clear: because the bank would not guarantee his exposure, he had decided to cease all spending on the strawberry crop and to simply abandon it.

A few days later we had a meeting with Peter Williams and I recounted this episode. Peter had not heard everything we said initially due to his hearing problem but he had worked out that this was a juicy story of a receiver in distress and he wanted to hear every last juicy moment of it. He turned his hearing aid up a notch and leant in over the table as I repeated an account of what had happened and the peculiar body language of Mike Greetham.

Peter leant back in his chair with a broad smile on his face and paused.

'Well I always maintained that Andersons were probably out of their depth on a case as complex as this' he said.

'It would clearly be quite reckless for a receiver not to see through on investments that had already been started on an imminent strawberry crop. The action he proposes, it would seem to me, is entirely against the interests of the creditors a receiver is meant to represent.

'In order to protect the interests of creditors, one option open to us would be to apply to the court for Mike Greetham and Andersons to be removed due to their incompetence and replaced with a Court Appointed Receiver who is able to do the job properly.'

'OK' I said, 'sounds good to me.'

I had put up with lots of derogatory comments from Andersons and Barclays about "poor performance" so now it was their turn. They had been at the helm for less than six months and had already got themselves in a muddle. They were totally out of their depth as far as I could see. We would get back on the front foot and turf out the receivers.

We issued a summons to the receivers and applied to the court for the removal of Andersons and their replacement with a Court Appointed Receiver. The Judge looked favourably on us. He commented that he thought the photos of the strawberry crop looked promising and that the good weather we had been having boded well. The Judge gave a clear steer that he was minded to grant the application and boot out the bank's chosen receivers. It would have been an abject humiliation for Andersons.

In order to avoid catastrophe, the bank caved in and Andersons conceded that they had acted wrongly and gave an undertaking to continue to fund the strawberry crop. They entered surrender negotiations with our legal team to agree terms before going back to court to finalise the agreement into a Court Order.

At last, we had something going our way. The final Order by Judge Jack at the end of May 1995 stated that my sons and I were to be, "entitled to do all things reasonably requisite for the management, preservation and harvest of the soft fruit crop at Bezurrel Farm and for the management and maintenance of the farm shop business at Trevaskis Farm."

It went on to require us to create a new account in our own names held by Barclays over which we would have full managerial control and it required the receivers to put a sum of money into that account for us to spend.

The receivers were, to all intents and purposes, turfed out of the business and would have no role in its day-to-day management. They were to revert to the position of dormant or sleeping receivers. It was a triumph for us and a humiliation for the bank.

Mike Greetham felt embittered by this experience and later told George, 'the Court Appointed Receiver thing was the final straw for me.' We didn't see him much after that. He tended to delegate all matters to Martin Redfearn and Richard Jackson. Although he felt humiliated by this defeat, the truth is he was also probably relieved. Barclays vs Eustice had been a bruising experience for Andersons and the strain was starting to show on their faces

Preparing for the main match

Siobhan Ward would be my barrister. She worked on the case all summer. I never met her or spoke to her. We had commissioned Grant Thornton, the big firm of accountants, to send two specialists, Duncan Swift and Nicholas Kidd, to look at the farm and the accounts and put forward the options that the Bank could have chosen other than Receivership. Duncan Swift of Grant Thornton would effectively be our expert witness. Redfearn, of Andersons, would appear in the same capacity for Barclays.

We had to get an independent valuation too. Burges Salmon always used Bruton Knowles. Their Keith Flemington knew me so well from the South Devon Herd Book Society that he was quite shocked by what the bank was doing. He put a value of around £1.2 million on our property, which was pretty much what we'd been led to believe before.

Barclays had already commissioned Stags, another West Country firm whose man did a hatchet job and came up with a figure of £728,000.

We were trying to run the farms in a way that would allow the business to continue after any trial. Our many acres of winter broccoli beds alone would be worth quite a bit of money. Even the seeds were expensive. I therefore decided to drill them somewhere else and asked Adele's father Cecil Olds, who was always prepared to share the benefits of whatever he had or did, to let me drill the seeds on his land. He was happy to help, so we took all our machinery down to St Buryan, prepared the field and I drilled them in one weekend. When they'd grown from seed we brought them back to plant on the farm. As a small way of showing our gratitude, we took our man down to St Buryan later in the summer and cut Cecil's silage for him.

All summer, George wrote letters for me to my MP, and the Chairman of the Bank, and all that came of it was reiteration of the Bank's position. They simply refused to discuss or negotiate at all. So we were going to have to take it all the way.

As part of our preparation for trial, we sought to get a leading barrister on board: David Neuberger QC who later became President of the Supreme Court. He had come recommended by Peter Williams.

During that summer, George and I drove to London and took a taxi from Paddington and walked under the arch of the gatehouse at Lincoln's Inn, past ancient brick and stone buildings to his Falcon Chambers. I don't remember what was said, so much as what Neuberger was like - friendly, but chaotic. I'd never seen a desk as messy as his, papers all over the place, and in the middle of the meeting he knocked a cup of coffee over the whole lot.

David Neuberger analysed our case forensically. He accepted that we had a moral case, but like Peter Williams almost a year earlier, confined his comments to our legal case. His view was that the strongest element of our case remained the breach of contract. He believed that, when it came to the tenancy agreements, the court had taken a "public policy decision' which was less about the law and more about what the courts thought should happen as a point of public policy. They had, he said, appeared to have formed the view that the law should be re-weighted in favour of the banks and away from what was provided for in statute in the 1925 Law of Property Act. As for the fact that the terms of our tenancies were incredibly generous and therefore contained no so called "ransom value", while it was a compelling argument, he believed the courts were ultimately saying that people should not be able to create such tenancies at all without the prior consent of the money lender and would find an excuse to find that way. So, we were to proceed with the breach of contract as our front line argument.

We had hoped that we would get David Neuberger to agree to be our barrister for the trial. Peter Williams felt that we had a good case on breach of contract albeit not a dead cert case. I think it was the main reason that Peter Williams thought we should meet David Neuberger ourselves. He had hoped that David Neuberger, having met us, might overcome any reservations and go for it. During July and August Peter Williams held a number of conversations with David Neuberger. He had been sold to us as someone who was willing to step in for the underdog in David v Goliath cases. Ours certainly measured up to that. However, we would need legal aid to be able to take things to trial and that needed the support of a serious barrister.

-

We had assembled a broad and experienced team to fight the bank, including the accountancy firm Grant Thornton. Peter Williams had told us that he believed the bank had been in operation politically to bring pressure to bear on some of the firms advising us. In particular, he said that he though Grant Thornton felt under pressure to caveat and water down their report. However, the final report from Grant Thornton, while not all we had hoped for, still said that Barclays should have known in 1992 that such a big loan would be difficult for us. They should never have advanced it but having done so, they should have stuck by us; yet they had never even considered many other options including the sale of other assets. Grant Thornton took apart the report prepared by Andersons. Furthermore, even as a worse case scenario, they pointed out that the option of a 'sleeping receiver', someone who essentially could have kept an eye on everything, and drive us through the tough times in case things went wrong.

I judged the South Devons at the Royal Welsh Show at Builth Wells that year. Jersey Growers carried on snooping whether I was at home or not. To me they were vultures, ready to pounce on everything our family had worked so hard to achieve. Once, when they turned up with Rudi Mock, Giles confronted them.

'This isn't your farm, so get off it. It's Eustice land and it always will be so go away.'

They left, muttering. We got travellers in to pick the strawberry crop at Bezurrel. We needed a big crowd, and they were the only ones we could find do the picking and pack-house work. We weren't supplying Kentish Garden any more, because they had decided to turn their backs on us, but we were sending soft fruit to Evesham instead.

The trial would take place before Judge Weeks at Bristol County Court in the second week of August; his draft judgement would be circulated maybe a month later, and the final version published after that. So we had a dilemma. We'd soon have to plant winter vegetables. We didn't want to give the bank any crops, so we had to grow them on land we thought we'd still be farming come the spring. Giles was due to start drilling in the middle of August and we'd already decided that if any land had to go it would be Bezurrel and Lemin. We'd leave them fallow.

One hot day that summer the BBC South West TV news programme, *Spotlight*, sent a reporter and crew to see us, and they broadcast a feature on our plight. After that we got more interest from television production companies, and a sympathetic half-page article and a big attention-grabbing photograph in the *Observer*. It was David and Goliath, really, and every reader would naturally sympathise with David. All the reporters were on our side. Our case illustrated a point about difficulties that farmers were having right across the region.

The Thursday before the trial we were trying to realise some cash from Bezurrel and Lemin. Trenowath Farm had been taken by David Piccaver, from Lincolnshire, and he'd got Jersey Growers over there planting daffodils already. George and I were surprised to see Mark Vandervliet himself, bulb-planting in the distance. We decided that pride was a luxury we couldn't afford, and crossed the field to talk to him personally and see if we could strike a deal on some of our land. We told him what we were thinking, but he wouldn't even talk about it. Wasn't interested in the slightest and said we had to leave.

When I got back home Peter Williams had left a message so I called him.

'We were over at Trenoweth trying to talk to Jersey Growers,' I said. 'You know, trying to strike a deal.'

'You shouldn't be talking to them,' he said 'you should be up here in Bristol talking to me. There's been a development. I want you to get here as soon as you can.'

'What is it?'

'Can you be here by four? I'd like to discuss it then. I'm sorry, but I have an appointment now.'

George, Giles Adele and I piled into my car and I drove all the way to his office in Bristol, a good three and a half hours away.

'I'm sorry this is going to be rather a blow to you all. The timing's terrible, but I'm afraid we have not been granted legal aid to continue with your case.' David Neuberger had not come through for us.

We were – well, dismayed doesn't cover it. It was a terrible blow.

'What! With three days to go? What do we do now?'

'Without a barrister, you have no hope of winning. So what I propose is this.'

He then lectured us as a family for half an hour on our 'options'. Peter reminded us that the intention had always been to buy time to get a settlement deal. The bank had apparently offered a limited tenancy on Tregotha but nothing else at all. None of the options appealed to me. Almost without exception they left us with very little. He even mentioned bankruptcy.

I felt that I had been taken down a winding road, at the end of which the only people to benefit would be the lawyers, while I would lose most of everything I had worked for all my life.

I was also conscious that the bank had been working politically on the senior partners of some of the blue chip firms advising us. Peter himself had told us that Grant Thornton were being got at by the bank. Was it the case that senior partners above Peter Williams in Burges Salmon were also being got at? Was Peter now under pressure from his own hierarchy to counsel for surrender?

So when Peter had listed all these options and summed up, he said:

'So what do you think, Paul?'

I just stared straight out of the window and said

'We're going to trial.'

'Paul, I'm afraid that's unwise and I can't advise you to do that. Even if you won this case, and the chance of that is very slim, they'd probably take further action. They could grind you down over time.'

It amounted to this. I might be a graduate of Harvard Business School and British Farmer of the Year, but none of that would matter because the bank would always have more money. That meant money to fight, year after year, whatever I chose to say and however many points I won.

I didn't see that, though. All I saw was my family, insulted and threatened.

'I don't see why. It's clear as day. They're in the wrong. They broke their promise. They haven't given us time to get our business straight. So whatever rights they thought they had, they were misusing.' I had faith in the British legal system. I thought the judge would see what seemed obvious to me. Above all, sympathetic publicity had only recently put me in good heart.

Peter was insistent.

Peter turned to George to ask him what he thought. Perhaps he hoped that George would be more emollient.

'I agree with all your analysis, Peter' said George. 'We had, indeed, always hoped to get a sensible settlement to this dispute and still do. However, perhaps the bank needs to see the whites of our eyes. We have nothing to lose by taking the bank over the brink. You also said when we first met that we needed to be robust enough and we are. We still have the opportunity after all of this to refight that rogue High Court decision in the Lords.'

Peter sighed.

'I can see I'm not going to shift you on this.' He was silent for a minute. Perhaps he genuinely thought we were wrong. Perhaps he was relieved that he had meticulously done what was required of him by his managing partners observed by the minute takers but we had dug in. We will never know.

'Well, George should act as the Litigant in Person. What do you say, George? You willing to stand up and be the barrister?'

George looked at me. I said nothing (always a good plan when you're surprised).

'All right,' he told Peter. 'Yes.'

'Good. Can you come in tomorrow for a briefing? I'll do what I can to prepare you. And then you can take Siobhan's paperwork home. Bring a car - you'll need one. '

George would represent us at the age of 22 and armed only with his Young Farmers Club debating skills.

-

The next day was Friday and George was up at the crack of dawn and on his way back to Bristol. I thought he'd be getting a crash course in court procedure and tricks of the advocate's trade. I didn't know for sure. I had never attended a High Court hearing, let alone one that was expected to last five days. On Friday night he brought back a car-boot load of files, all inches thick, containing not only our discovery documents but the other side's. We hadn't seen those previously.

George worked on the files – he'd learned to call them bundles – all weekend and Giles helped him. Discovery is revelation: a series of surprises. It was the first time we saw what the bank were really saying about us behind our back in the year running up to the breakdown in relations. We saw that their preferred option was a "winding down" of the business, that they regarded the appointment of Andersons as a box ticking "due diligence exercise" and that they regarded our case as, essentially, "a duel between the solicitors" i.e. Bond Pearce and Burges Salmon.

Until Thursday afternoon George had never imagined that he might have to conduct cross-examination. As usual he was up for any amount of work. In support of his arguments, he would have to refer to a particular page in a given file so that he, and the Barclays barrister, and the Judge, would be looking at the same document. Giles would act as his Junior that week, listening carefully, taking a note if necessary, and passing him papers from the bench behind, as each reference was raised in

151

court. George would need a sharp mind, an accurate memory and an eye for detail, because he had to know how to draw what he wanted out of witnesses on both sides. The Barclays legal team would have perceived weaknesses in our own arguments and George had to be ready to respond with an equally well targeted attack on the bank. He knew, and in many cases had written, the evidence we'd submitted ourselves, but he hadn't read everything Barclays disclosed before.

He had to grasp all this on Friday night and Saturday and Sunday.

Des Phillips had booked us into a hotel in Sedgemoor from Sunday night to Friday morning. On Monday morning early, we left our hotel and drove to Bristol hoping to fix up a negotiation with Bond Pearce 'on the steps of the court'. Des, who seemed to have wide experience of court hearings, was sure that Bond Pearce would advise Barclays to settle and the hearing would be called off.

He was wrong. I know now that Bond Pearce were unlikely to advise Barclays of any such thing because this was their one, and perhaps only, chance to prove themselves to Barclays and perhaps permanently displace Burges Salmon as the preferred solicitor for the South West.

We carried the bundles into the Old High Court building. All week, we'd take them back to the hotel and work on them together in the evenings.

Our case was heard in a traditional courtroom panelled in dark wood with a big coat of arms on the end wall above the Judge's bench. We took seats on one side of the court while George and Giles arranged the bundles on the benches in the middle where the barristers sat. Trolley-loads of files were trundled in. Everybody was bustling about in dark suits with a job to do.

The Barclays barrister was a QC. He wore a wig and gown and had no less than four other junior lawyers supporting him.

Peter had told me I could expect to be cross-examined by Barclays' lead barrister and that he would try to dent my confidence. I didn't think my confidence could be 'dented' since I knew our case was right.

In no time the clerk of the court called 'All rise' – and as we stood up, Judge Weekes, also in wig and gown, walked onto the platform from a side door and took his place behind the bench.

We all sat down. The morning was taken up with the Plaintiffs' barrister's opening remarks, that is, an outline of their case. The Judge had already read witness statements from both sides, including mine.

Barclays' barrister, a haughty little man called Davies, described our situation in dark words. Inadequate planning had led to our overspend on setting up the strawberry fields. Misjudgement, mismanagement, and generally misplaced enthusiasm had led to the Partnership's appearance here today. (There wasn't a lot said about the weather.) He painted a picture of profligate spending, forever just under or over the overdraft limit, and careless farming – which couldn't have been further from the truth.

According to him, Barclays would probably have continued to throw good money after bad if John Bloor hadn't heard alarm bells when I mentioned Burges Salmon.

That day, and on subsequent days, we had to listen to all this. Their significant witnesses were Vague, Bloor, Hammond and Redfearn. George cross-examined without emotion, as he'd been told to. I can't remember exactly what anybody said in court but I can give you a flavour of it . I know slow-spoken Vague provided a moment of levity when George asked him a question.

'That's bank secrets, that is. Can't tell you that.'

The Judge looked amused. 'This is a court of law, Mr Vague. There are no secrets here.'

I felt sorry for the poor fellow.

George put it to Bloor, in particular, that he'd made up his mind what he wanted the men from Andersons to tell him even before they went there. Bloor denied it.

George read out the brief with which Andersons had been supplied. Bloor denied responsibility.

'It was my Regional office that sent that to Mr Redfearn.'

George asked Bloor to explain what he meant by "winding down" which is what he had said he wanted to do well in advance of appointing Andersons. The question was dodged.

-

George also asked him to describe what was meant by 'A.K.A "due diligence"' when internal memos discussed the real purpose for appointing Andersons. Bloor professed ignorance of what the term meant.

Redfearn stepped into the witness box. George asked about the results from the farm last spring.

'Were those results any better than those of the previous year, when Paul Eustice was running the farm?'

'No.'

'Worse?'

'About the same.'

'You have impressive qualifications, Mr Redfearn. Why do you think the farm had a relatively poor performance when you were in charge?'

'The weather, largely.'

'Pretty much the same as when Paul Eustice was in charge, then. Thank you, Mr Redfearn.'

Standing up in court George was forthright and aggressive and put them on the back foot. I thought he did a brilliant job, and Giles supported him the way nobody else could have. I was proud of both of them. Serena came down from Shropshire whenever she could, which was wonderful. Without Adele beside me and our children's support this trial would have destroyed me. A lot of old friends had faded away by this time.

I think it was Thursday when we got a chance to defend ourselves. George, in his opening remarks, did a great job for us. He painted a picture of the Partnership's success until 1992; the circumstances around our cautious purchase of Bezurrel, and our new relationship with Barclays. He told the court that I had borrowed from them because although I had told them to expect a rocky start they'd willingly undertaken to support us with a loan payable over the next twenty years. None of us doubted that they would hold to that, especially since the loan was guaranteed by nearly a million pounds' worth of property. I had had to spend far more than we expected, or wanted, to establish the strawberries, which thrived in their first year.

But after less than twelve months, Barclays had aggressively demanded agricultural securities and reneged on the mortgage, making it a one-year on demand loan. And eleven months later they brought in people from Andersons who began their work by making an inventory. Unsurprisingly, this deepened my suspicion that they were lining us up for receivership. On top of constant unhelpful pressure and demands for paperwork, these intrusions – plus advice from third parties – made me seek legal advice. The Partnership needed breathing space if it's winter and spring operations were to come good, so acting on advice I'd created the tenancies. There was never any intent to defraud - just to delay further clumsy intervention. I was trying to get through this to benefit both the Partnership and the bank. But within 24 hours of Bloor knowing I had sought professional legal advice, the bank had foreclosed.

Adele and I both felt quite emotional that day; over-awed by the competence and loyalty of all our children. Whatever came next, we were a strong unit.

We summoned Bernard Pooley back from a holiday in the Canary Islands to testify that he'd supplied nearly all the G Eustice & Son figures and reports in 1993-94 at Barclays' request. They had been talking to him, not us.

He wasn't best pleased to be called back to England, although it didn't cost him much except a couple of missed days on the beach.

The part I hated most was being cross-examined by their QC, Stephen Davies. He peered at me as if I was some sort of insect and had a typically haughty manner.

'Mr Eustice, I see your plans were turned down twice by the National Westminster Bank....

'....Frankly they didn't think your farm plan was strong enough to sustain more lending, did they, Mr Eustice?

'.....Mr Eustice, your business was struggling, was it not, when you borrowed from Barclays?

'Mr Eustice...

I don't know what he hoped to achieve, except to undermine me, which I suppose is a tactic barristers use. It seemed plain as day to me that if Barclays hadn't thoroughly combed through our accounts, they wouldn't have taken us on. They hadn't been lending money to a struggling farmer. I was a farmer who wanted to extend his business and prosper and who had a good idea for a way to do it. Somehow Davies engineered his questions so that I didn't get a chance to make this clear.

'I put it to you, Mr Eustice, that in October of 1994 you knew that you would not be able to meet your commitments before Christmas. Was that so?

'We were –'

'Just a yes or no will be adequate. Did you honestly think that you would be able to pay your bills, and the bank, in October?'

'Not in full but we –'

'Thank you Mr Eustice. No, you did not think you would be able to pay the bank.'

'No it's not. I only wanted time to run my farm. Farming's up and down all the time and Barclays had reassured me. They'd told me they were in it for the long haul but I didn't trust them any more after they got Andersons in.'

'I don't seem to have heard an answer to my question, Mr Eustice,' he sneered. 'Let's begin with the basics, shall we? Why do you think the Bank holds securities against the loan?'

And so on it went, with this man who deployed a patronising manner as a weapon. Question after question designed to make me look wily and devious.

I was sitting in the witness box, occasionally sipping water, for a whole morning answering questions. George, as a witness, had to confront Davies as well.

Davies also launched a personal attack on Peter Williams and, in particular, Des Phillips. On one morning his team arrived at the court before proceedings started and handed out a transcript of a BBC radio report into Des Phillip's business past.

"Are you aware of a BBC radio report into Des Phillips' affairs?" he shouted in his supercilious tone.

'Yes, you gave me a copy of a transcript this morning.' I replied.

Davies blushed and felt foolish. For a brief moment his characteristic haughtiness was absent.

It is worth dwelling on the position as far as Des Phillips and Peter Williams from Burges Salmon are concerned. Des Phillips had a chequered past. He had made mistakes. He had got himself into positions, which meant he had ended up letting people down. To some, both at the time and, inevitably, since, he would be regarded as something of a rogue - not to put too finer point on it. Indeed, when Judge Weeks gave his Judgement he used words to this effect.

Peter Williams, for his part, prided himself on being a litigator rather than just a solicitor. He was a street fighter. He was rather vain at times. He was not your usual, risk averse solicitor trying to keep his nose clean. He was bright and would contemplate creative manoeuvres to deliver an outcome for his clients. He took the bank's bean when working for the bank but you got the impression that he rather relished working for the underdog where he could.

The reality is that the world of insolvency is what it is and the same types of people act on either side. We did not ask to be here. We did everything we could to avoid it. We repeatedly offered to meet and discuss and negotiate but the bank refused. In the end, you have to fight fire with fire.

And what about the banks? With their dubious dawn raids run by people of dubious character; their ruses to force sell unwanted insurance products; their payment of "permanent retainers" to top flight legal firms to ensure they are conflicted out of acting against them and to deny their customers access to good legal advice and their threatening undertones about future business prospects to those professionals who have the courage to act against them. The banks are not morally superior.

I didn't learn much that was new that week. Some suspicions were confirmed. Bloor was slippery about the reassurances he had given me at the start. The bank appeared to have a clear agenda that was being discussed internally to "wind down" the business. The appointment of Andersons was, implicitly, something of a sham exercise to demonstrate "due diligence."

Bloor had raised the alarm with Risk Management, Irons' department, as soon as I mentioned that I wanted a meeting with my solicitors present. It's a curious thing when something as simple as a customer consulting a serious firm of solicitors is judged as reason to foreclose but that is what appeared to happen within the senior management of Barclays Bank.

On Friday, Davies summed up the Bank's challenge to the tenancies. George challenged the legitimacy of the bank's claim against us because they had ordered Andersons to come steaming in just nine months after the loan was agreed. He emphasised the unfair treatment we had received and the foolishness of the panic behind the bank's attitude. George had again drawn attention to bank memos revealing that the bank had an agenda to "wind down" the business contrary to what they maintained in the court. He also drew attention to the memo where the appointment of Andersons was described as "A.K.A due diligence". Witnesses appearing for the bank had all professed ignorance as to what "A.K.A" meant but it means "also known as" and it was clear from the context that this was internal code or banter within the bank to describe a sham exercise to demonstrate "due diligence" for no more than presentational or legal reasons.

It was all over by lunchtime. When we walked out into the warm August day I saw Davies and the Barclays team vanishing into a nearby pub for lunch. I think we had a meal with Des. After that we drove home. It was over. Judge Weeks would deliver his draft judgement in about four weeks' time. Des

Phillips thought we'd probably be invited to negotiate before then, anyway.

Judgement day

A month later, on the day in September 1995 when Judge Weeks would issue his verdict at the court, Peter Williams and Des Phillips came with us. We took our seats as before. Somebody from Bond Pearce was there.

'All rise.'

We sat, we listened, as the Judge read out quite a long report. It described, briefly, matters as they had been before we moved our accounts to Barclays: the family in the landscape, the Partnership, the overdraft with the Natwest; my father's death; my uncle's need to sell up; our eventual decision to ask the Natwest for a mortgage on Bezurrel, where we would grow strawberries. The fact that the Natwest declined.

'With hindsight this was probably a sensible decision,' he said. I didn't like the sound of that.

And so it went on, an account of how the Partnership was awarded a loan and overdraft. As to Tregotha 'Mr Paul Eustice says, *and I accept*, that he had completely forgotten the lease, the purpose of which had been to save tax on his father's death. It did not occur to him to mention it to the two bank managers.' Good. Davies had questioned my honesty about that. But it had been ignored by everyone, that lease. This whole matter of Barclays' charge over Tregotha was important but confusing. I just wanted the Judge, right now, to tell Barclays to leave my mother in her home.

On and on went the Judge, summarising the case in detail.

'Mr George Eustice, who has presented the family case with great skill,' said the Judge in giving his verdict 'has relied on these notes to submit that the bank had a closed mind and a firm intention to appoint receivers, possibly even before

Andersons were appointed, and certainly by the time the family took their defensive action on the nineteenth of November. I do not find that this is so.'

My heart sank. *I do not find that this is so.* He was going to come down on their side.

The Judge droned on. My attention wandered. I thought of the cows, and the pigs, and the harvest. About how I'd worked when the children were little, and after a long summer's day Adele and I would drive them down to the beach near her father's place sometimes, with a picnic, and they'd play on the warm sand and fish about in rock pools until dusk.

Judge Weeks was talking about Tregotha, the tenancies, and something called Estoppel. There were a lot of ins and outs and quotes from other cases but in his legal judgement the bank held Tregotha, and our tenancy, as its security. They could do what they liked with it. This came as a great surprise to the bank's own lawyers who had assumed they had lost that argument.

That was us finished, then. My mother would have to leave her home. I consider that to have been a big failure on Judge Weeks' part and when I heard that, I lost faith in British Justice. His judgement was thorough in some respects but I felt that he had failed to take due account of the key internal memos from the bank where it was clear that their agenda was to "wind down" the business and where the appointment of Andersons was described as little more than a presentational exercise.

However, there were a few positives. 'I find Mr Eustice and his sons to be entirely honourable persons. They acted, as they saw it, to protect the financial interests of the family and they did so in accordance with the advice of solicitors of the highest repute....'

We retained our good name, but little else. I felt very, very disappointed. The Judge had found for the Bank.

Peter Williams said to me, 'That's it, we've had it.'

We left, despondent. Out in the street I said 'What'll they do next, Des?'

'Oh,' he said 'I've seen it before. They'll give you time to sort yourselves out and start feeling safe, and then they'll come in suddenly and clear you out.'

Negotiations begin

However, it was not over yet. Barclays Bank were conscious that they had relied quite heavily in the trial on documents that were disclosed by virtue of the Court of Appeal decision earlier in the summer, regarding legal privilege, which had surprisingly gone their way, but it was a judgement that was not considered safe.

The Law Society were open to sponsoring an appeal to the House of Lords. If, as expected, the bank were to lose that appeal in the Lords then they would be back to square one.

So, having won the trial but feeling exposed, the bank were open to negotiating a settlement. I had been tempted to say let's fight on and go to the Lords. However, George argued that this was the one window where we had negotiating leverage and should aim to land a deal.

There were a number of rounds of discussions about what a settlement might look like. At one point we almost secured agreement that we could buy back all of the farms under preferential terms in return for discontinuing legal action and drawing a line under the dispute. In fact, the regional director of Barclays, when presented with this option said "we are not a million miles apart." However, other advisers in the room looked worried and hurriedly adjourned the meeting and asked for some private space.

In the event, the fact that the Jersey growers were waiting in the wings meant that securing a deal that included Bezurrel as well as all the other farms was not achievable but we settled on a deal that left Barclays with some of the land while we retained the balance. The precise terms of the deal were to remain confidential so I will not disclose them here. Heads of terms were agreed. The only remaining sticking point was how long we needed to raise the money to refinance the operation.

Peter Williams was clear that we needed to have a reasonable amount of time to refinance, otherwise the whole deal could fall apart. There were therefore on-going discussions about the final timings of payments needed to bank the settlement agreement. In the meantime, we started to work up new business plans with a view to securing finance from an alternative bank.

The eye of the storm

With the uncertainty around the future of the business, George and Giles started to consider other alternative enterprises that could supplement the core business we planned to refinance. Early in November George saw an ad in the paper: Gabbons Nurseries, where they grew tomatoes in greenhouses over in Penryn, was up for rental. George said

'I could grow early strawberries under glass over there. What do you think, Dad?'

'I'd go for it. At the end of the day, George, it may be all you're left with.'

So he went ahead, rang the owner, and developed the idea on paper. A couple of nights later I was with George at Gabbons Nurseries talking about the deal with the owner, Neville Gambier, when Adele rang me on my mobile.

Martin had called from Wadebridge. A friend of his who'd been at Wadebridge Market that day had told him somebody, he wasn't sure who, had been looking for drovers to go to West Cornwall and load cattle tomorrow, at Gwinear, on behalf of a bank. Martin thought it might be our herd.

I said

'Barclays would never do that would they? We have agreed heads of terms on a deal. The only residual discussion is over timings. Why on earth would they now consider trying to come in and seize everything?'

By the time we had returned home later that evening, Adele had received two more phone calls from concerned cattle drovers who had received the same call about a job in Gwinear the following morning. It was reassuring that the farming community in Cornwall knew whose side they were on even as they were being offered money by the bank to betray their fellow Cornishman.

Adele had also called Peter Williams to report these strange reports to him. She said he was cagey and reluctant to speak but did say it wouldn't surprise him based on a rather terse letter he had received from the bank that evening. He was unable to offer any constructive advice as to what we should do.

'We will just have to wait and see' he said.

It beggared belief that Barclays might be about to renege on an agreement for the second time but the intelligence was too consistent to be ignored. Any action by them to seize assets would have been in breach of the heads of terms already agreed. If this was an attempt by the bank to pretend that they had engaged in discussion only to then petulantly come in and seize everything then that behaviour warranted a response.

I had about 150 cows and calves at Tregotha, and twelve or fifteen steers at Bezurrel. How to get them away, and where to put them? We racked our brains.

Many friends from the local farming community were willing to help. One in particular gave invaluable help at an hour of desperate need. He and his brother were cattle farmers and they had a big double-decker lorry. I told him what Adele had heard from Martin.

'I think they're coming to pick up all my cattle tomorrow. It sounds very much like it and I want to move them but I'm desperate and I don't know what to do. Would you move them for me?'

'Well I would, but the lorry's not here.' 'I've got a load of cattle off the market coming in there tomorrow and my driver's back here, he's just gone home, he's got an early start... How big's the herd?'

'About 150.'

'Where are they?'

'The cows are out running and the calves are in the sheds.'

He whistled a bit but I knew he was thinking about it.

'Look,' he said. 'If you can get your cattle into the yard over at Tregotha, I'll fetch the lorry myself and get them into lairage facilities. But you've got to find somewhere else tomorrow.'

I knew I'd have at least an hour before he brought the lorry to Tregotha. I got back in the car and went to see another life-long friend from the farming community locally. I sat down and told him what was going on and his phone rang in the hall. His wife was giving me a cup of tea when he came back into the room.

'Well, what you say is right. That was David. John May rang him and asked if he'd help round your cattle up. He wanted me to let you know.'

'*John May?*' John had been a friend over the years. Now I knew why he made that snide remark about the boys having a whip-round for the rent. He must be working for the bank, probably through Andersons. 'Well, I might have known. What do you – '

'Paul we've got to make a move. I'll come out and bring 'em in with you. I can keep a few in our shed as well.'

That's what a true friend is.

We both drove over to Tregotha; must have got there about 11pm. George and Giles turned up, and Alan Cook, and Anthony Mitchell who'd lived at Angarrack Hill Farm before I sold it. Six of us. Quietly, in dim moonlight, we fanned out across the fields and gently herded the cows towards the yard. Ten, twenty, thirty cattle, ahead of us, with that strange lolloping, swaying walk they have. Docile creatures, a couple of the younger ones frisking at the edge of the group. We got about sixty in, then did it again, and three of us were rounding up a few stragglers when we saw dipped headlights rocking softly down the lane, and heard the rumble of the double-decker.

The lorry backed up and we got about a third of them inside. He took that load over to holding facilities, then came back for another, and then came back and took the yearlings over to the big shed on another friend's farm. Before that last trip out of Tregotha he said to me

'What about your steers over Bezurrel?'

'No, too frisky. We won't get them in tonight. I've got some lovely heifers on that rented land at Kehelland. They'll be all right tonight but I've got to find a place for them soon.'

'Right. And the pigs? Where are your pigs?'

'There's only a few here. We're feeding them for the farm shop. I already took my sows down to Helston to a relative.'

The next day was Friday. I was desperate to get the heifers out of Kehelland and over to a safe site that week so I rang Alan from the phone box.

'No it's all right Paul, they're over there already. Him and me took'em first thing this morning.'

I could have danced a jig. What friends I had. They hadn't wanted me to be seen moving the heifers, so they'd both gone up to Kehelland at first light. It's high land and they'd driven the cows, there were about thirty of them, out of the gate, down a tree-shaded tarmac road into the valley, and turned off to safety.

So Giles and George were with me at Tregotha that Friday morning expecting Andersons to turn up. We thought that "dawn raid" might have literally meant what it said but we waited and waited. Then we heard the aggressive sound of a convoy of lorries roaring down the road.

'Here we go.' I said.

'I will head out to meet them at the end of the lane' said my younger son, Giles.

'What will you tell them?'

Giles had a mischievous look on his face.

'Well, none of those articulated lorries will be able to turn around in the yard. So I might just invite them all to drive up the lane together. Then we can enjoy watching them reverse back out empty handed.'

When Mike Greetham, the receiver reached the end of the lane he asked where all the cattle were.

'There's none here.'

'What d'you mean? Where are they!'

'Well, we got short of grazing and I had to move them out onto fresh ground.'

He looked furious.

'They were here at ten-thirty last night. They must still be here. Where have you put them?' The bank's men had placed all the farms under surveillance just as our planning had predicted. But they gave up and went to bed after a certain hour, which was also predictable.

'They're not here. You can go out and look for yourself.'

'That's exactly what I intend to do.'

He walked all over Tregotha and Bezurrel to look for the cattle but there was not one animal left on the farm. I got a call; there were two more lorries waiting at Bezurrel. Somebody had seen John May at the roundabout at Camborne, directing the whole convoy towards our farms.

Greetham came back in a temper. 'You won't get away with this, Eustice! We are entitled to seize assets! Where are they.'

'It's OK, they are safe.'

While he ranted I was thinking of one time in our office when I'd told him we'd win and I trusted British justice would prevail and he'd said something like

'Well best of luck with that. What a judge decides can depend on whether or not he had good sex the night before.'

I knew I could find out exactly what he said because I'd got a recording of it, word for word. He was still going on at me.

'What the hell have you done with the cattle?'

I wouldn't say. He followed me into our kitchen. He stayed there for hours, alternately threatening and encouraging, but nothing made any difference. About midday there was a knock at the back door and I opened it to a policeman.

'Er... hallo Mr Eustice. Is everything all right?'

'Yes.'

'You have a Mr Greetham with you?'

'Yes, you want to talk to him? Come in.'

The policeman was in and out within two minutes. Somebody from Andersons must have decided to check in case I was holding the Receiver hostage with a double-barrelled shotgun. Nothing could have been further from my thoughts. Time was going on and by 3 o'clock I could only think about where to take my cattle, and how to find a lorry.

I made an excuse and got out into the yard. George and Giles were there.

'He's still in the kitchen,' I said 'I'm off out to move the cows. Whatever you do don't let him take those steers off Bezurrel.'

Shortly afterwards, George received a phone call from Peter Sawdon who was one of the regional directors at Barclays Bank. George had established a good working relationship with Peter Sawdon and had worked closely with him to develop the heads of terms for the settlement agreement. There was a surprising amount of goodwill given the acrimony of the previous nine months. However, on both sides, that was now out the window.

'WHERE ARE THE CATTLE!' screeched Peter Sawdon.

'They are very safe. Don't worry, we have it all under control.' replied George.

'THIS IS AN OUTRAGE! THE BANK IS ENTITLED TO THESE ASSETS!'

'Why are you doing this?' replied George. 'We had a deal. This just makes no sense.'

Sawdon fell silent since he had no explanation for the bank reneging on the agreement under discussion.

George gave an undertaking to speak to Peter Williams in order to get Peter Sawdon off the phone and to then come back to him.

George then phoned Peter Williams and explained the situation.

'I know you told my mother yesterday evening that we had no option but to wait and see what happened until this morning. However, at around 11.30 last night, we became concerned about the quality of the grazing here at Tregotha, so we made some changes.'

"hmm.'

'We now have a surprising situation where the bank have attempted a bungled dawn raid and their Regional Director, Peter Sawdon and the receivers are screaming at us and saying we need to take them to the cattle.'

Peter paused. And then said, 'This is obviously a stressful turn of events for everyone concerned and there is a lot of anger and stress in the air from those representing the bank. I think the best thing is for everyone to go home and have a weekend to cool down and then we can re-engage in discussions next week. Perhaps you might suggest to the bank that they contact me to arrange a discussion next week but it sounds very much to me that everyone would benefit from having a weekend off.'

George did this.

There was a cattle lorry backed up to the field gate over at Bezurrel already. I didn't know what I was going to do about all my cows filling the pens at the James' brothers' farm but I had to find another transporter and then I wasn't sure where I could move them to.

I drove off with my mobile in my pocket but I didn't dare use it. I was sure that if I made a call Andersons, or the bank's security department, would be able to listen in or at least track where I was. I was looking for Neil, the contractor who was doing my haulage at the time and he only had a small lorry but if he was willing to help, we'd manage somehow. So I switched my phone off and drove to his cottage near Helston. I knocked on the door but there was no reply. I was turning away when Joe, another farmer friend whose farm abutted this lane, came along in his pickup.

He stopped and we said hello.

'I'm looking for Neil,' I said. 'But there's no answer. He must be away somewhere.'

'Oh, no, Neil doesn't live here any more. He lives over your way, at Horsedown.... Can I help?'

I told him of my predicament and that I had to move the cows somewhere else because of what had happened and they were trying to strip me out. 'Don't you worry about it,' Joe said. 'I'll keep those cows as long as you need.'

'Joe, you've just saved my life. If you can do that - but I've got to move them. If I could find Neil we could move 'em tonight. Have you got a number for him?'

'No but he definitely lives at Horsedown. Go over there and ask.'

I knew Horsedown and there are only about eight houses in it, so when I got there and saw Neil's lorry parked outside one of them I knew I'd struck lucky.

Neil was happy to help. How could I have done any of this without such good friends? My farmer friend was relieved when I told him I'd found a place to put them. I managed to get hold of Neil anyhow; he came with me that evening and helped load them up. Neil's lorry could only take about twelve at a time and we were back and forth, back and forth like a machine. Getting them all down to Joe's at Helston took the whole long dark evening. When I left the very last load it was about eleven at night and I said to Joe

'I'll come down in the week with fodder for 'em.'

'If I were you,' he said, 'I'd keep away. Get somebody else to come over. They'll be looking out for you.' He was right. But we did have plenty of straw in one of our barns, and a friend of George's loaded a big stack of it onto a tractor trailer and got it down to him after dark. The cattle were there for about a month.

I dropped Neil back at Horsedown and drove back to Trevaskis, where George and Giles were still up. There'd been developments.

Jack Harvey Plant Hire from Truro had arrived not long after I left. They brought a couple of low loaders to pick up our farm machinery and take it away. Jack Harvey was well known locally as a nasty piece of work and some years later would land up in prison for a multitude of criminal offences.

But today, we was employed by Barclays Bank. I was very proud of our ERF lorry. We'd left it safe but they smashed the windows and the steering lock, and had to tow it back to Truro.

They took all my tractors, and a whole catalogue of other machinery, most of which they managed to wreck before it was out of the yard. They also stole the tools from my workshop, which had nothing to do with the farm at all. I never saw those again.

At the height of the altercation, my son Giles was parked outside of the Mace shop at Reawla observing the receivers. A group of children from the village came up to him and said, 'we have heard what these people are doing. Is there anything we can do to help? We want to help.' It was extraordinary the way the community closed ranks against the actions of the bank and their agents. Initially Giles said 'Thanks very much, but I don't think there is much you can do.'

Then he had an idea.

'Actually, here's an idea. You see that car over there. They are the enemy trying to steal everything we have. Take this five pound note. Go into the Mace shop and buy some eggs. Whoever scores the most hits gets to keep the change.'

Later that day, Giles resumed surveillance of the receiver's car to see that an egg shell was lodged in the rear view wiper.

Alan Cook had been there and seen all the reprehensible actions of Jack Harvey and his thugs. I think Mike Greetham must have told Harvey what he wanted from us, but if Greetham was still there when the low loaders came, he did a terrible job of supervision.

'Have we still got the steers at Bezurrel?' I asked, without much hope.

'You bet. The lorry turned up and the travellers went over whooping and hollering and waving towels and the cattle were bounding about all over the field. Those guys couldn't have driven them to the gate, let alone loaded them.'

That was one up for us. But I still didn't know where to put the steers if I shifted them. It had been a long day.

Jack Harvey turned up at Trevaskis again the following morning. This time he brought his two burly daughters. They intended to pick up more equipment so they had a low loader parked on the road. It was too big to go down our lane, which goes steeply down, then rises again, and there's a railway bridge across the dip at the bottom – a low bridge that their lorry couldn't get under. So what Jack Harvey did, he went down the lane and under the bridge with a digger, filled the scoop with equipment, and tried to drive it back up.

Richard Jackson, Martin Redfearn's usual companion, turned up as well. Adele stopped him on his way down to the farm. He lowered his window.

'Good morning Mrs Eustice.'

Adele leaned towards him. 'Where are you going?'

'Down to Trevaskis.'

'No you're damn well not.' Before he knew what was happening she'd reached in and snapped off the ignition key in the lock.

My wife is about five feet three and eight stone. To this day she doesn't know how she did that. She says sheer fury gave her a rush of adrenalin.

The car was stranded. Jackson was stranded. I saw him using his phone.

A few moments later, with Richard Jackson from Andersons at the end of the lane watching, three pick up loads of New Age travellers swept through the entrance having come over from Bezurrel and headed down the lane in pursuit of Harvey.

Richard Jackson phoned Mike Greetham on his mobile and said, 'It's getting a bit out of hand here.'

'Continue!' barked Greetham down the phone line from the comfort of his Leicestershire home.

'Continue?' queried Richard.

Richard Jackson was the nicest of the Anderson people. To be fair to him he didn't enjoy this element of the job. He wanted to do genuine farm consultancy for genuine farm businesses and was never very comfortable getting his hands grubby for the bank. In that respect he was different to both Martin Redfearn and Mike Greetham. But here, on the day of mayhem, he was ordered in on his own while the other two retreated for a weekend off, barking orders down the phone at him.

Richard Jackson turned to the local Police Officer who had been asked to attend in support to ask whether he could attend with him.

'Sorry mate, I can only get involved after there has been physical violence, not before.'

Richard Jackson's face fell.

The Police behaved in an incredibly professional way throughout. They knew our family and had worked with us to catch thieves and tackle burglaries over the years but they had a job to do. However, they were equally clear that their job did not extend to giving free security to receivers or the bank.

Jack Harvey's two daughters came into the restaurant and Adele ordered them out, which was brave of her because they were chips off the old block, both of them. Foul-mouthed, rough and nasty women. They had to sit in the lorry on the road, smoking, effing and blinding, and chucking dog-ends out of the window.

I kept an eye on the car park and Richard Jackson's car. About an hour later an AA van drove in. The driver was Francis Williams. I'd known him for years; he was happy to service and repair our lorries sometimes. So I walked over and

'What brings you here Francis?'

'I got this car to get going again', he said.

'I shouldn't do too much to that car if I were you,' I said 'because that's the Receiver's, and he's got Jack Harvey here trying to strip out all my machinery this morning.'

'Well I got to have a look at it,' he said. He went over and spoke to Richard Jackson and fiddled about with the ignition and then he walked back and I said,

'Well, what about it then Francis?'

'I can't do anything about that,' he said, and left. So the Receiver was stuck with his car in the middle of our driveway unable to move it.

We gave Jack Harvey such a bruising that Saturday morning that he decided to leave empty handed. He slunk off with the Receiver's car on the back of the low loader and him and his two daughters, and the Receiver, sitting in the cab at the front.

We all laughed, although we were feeling very sad at the time.

They never came back to the farm to try to grab any more farm equipment. They never came back to try to get any more of our livestock. We quietly got the steers off Bezurrel the following week. Some other friends and family collected them in the dark one night and took them to a farm near Padstow. A van followed the first thirty miles away from Bezurrel but it turned off at Truro.

The bank went on making enquiries. They must have sent a memo round all the branches in West Cornwall. That week, one of the friend who had helped me was asked by his bank manager:

'What have you done with the Eustices' cattle?'

And his brother-in-law said to him:

'You've got a lot more cattle than you used to have. I never thought you had as many as this.'

So I felt uneasy. People talk; they mean no harm but they talk. Things were getting a bit hot and knowing that most farmers depend on the good will of their banks, I didn't want my friends to risk their livelihoods by hiding my cattle much longer.

Des did me a favour. That week, he arranged a place in North Devon where I could board them at a reasonable rate. I went up to see it and it was fine. The farmer was a nice fellow who knew what he was doing. My cousin Martin and I organised transport and we went over to all the relevant farms and sent all the heifers up there first thing one morning.

That night Martin called from Wadebridge, laughing.

'I don't believe this. Have you got the TV on?'

'No what is it?'

'Oh it's gone now... It's your cows. They've just been on Spotlight. There was a bad accident on the A30 this morning and they got stuck in the tailback. I saw that bloody great lorry with the name on it and then there was a close-up shot, and you could see the cows through the vents looking out.'

'Were they OK?'

'Yes they're fine, they just got stuck in a jam. Here's us, taking all this trouble to keep things quiet, and your cattle get themselves on television.'

At last, the deal was done

My cousins, my uncle, my friends, my farm workers; many people went out of their way to help us and I can never repay loyalty like that. Adele's sister Charmaine once lent me £600 out of her own pocket to pay a bill. She was a wonderful woman. Adele's customers were tremendous as well, always asking after our welfare, and the restaurant was very well supported. But we were in limbo, really, and had been since the trial ended in August.

Barclays and Alder King, the Receivers, were also stuck. Bad publicity on the farming grapevine was not what they wanted and, rather than behaving honourably, they had been petulant and things had backfired on them spectacularly. They were now in a worse position than ever. So, negotiations resumed. The heads of terms were the same but this time we managed to agree timelines and deadlines for securing various components.

We agreed that that they would have occupation of some of the farms, such as Bezurell and Lemin, to sell and we would have an arrangement to raise funds to purchase back the remainder such as Tregotha, Trevaskis and Angrarrack. I would get my equipment back on loan so I'd be able to farm Trevakis, Tregotha and Angarrack Hill over the winter and we would own the winter crops on all the farms until cleared.

I thought another bank would surely be willing to give us a securitised loan against Trevaskis, the restaurant and shop and Tregotha and Angarrack.

To raise working capital we sent some cattle to Gloucester market in December. I had to keep the bloodline going, but if I could sell some of the cows, the money would ensure that I kept the rest.

We were hanging onto our land by our fingertips. We'd got vegetables in the ground, so we'd have a crop to sell next summer, and we'd got our South Devons back with us, and the British Lops that I'd taken to my uncle at Helston. He was another one who'd stuck his neck out to help me. Now we needed our lorry and the farm machinery to work with. Peter Thomas, a local farm equipment supplier, was kind enough to drive his low loader up to Truro and collect a lot of my tools and machinery from Jack Harvey. I went up to his yard myself one evening and knocked on his office door to ask for some of my equipment that I couldn't find. He came to the door and told me I couldn't have it. I asked where my stuff was and he started swearing and threatening me with a swing wrench.

I was out of there fast, but the day after, I rang Greetham and told him what had happened.

'He said he's been told to keep it until I'm allowed to go and get it. When's that going to be?'

'I've no idea. I dare say George has it recorded somewhere.'

I never did understand why Barclays Bank, or Andersons, got mixed up with a crook like Harvey. Fourteen years later, he was found guilty of receiving stolen goods and intimidating a rival firm. He'd lost out to another company on a contract, so he set fire to seven pieces of plant they owned – including a lorry with the driver asleep in the cab. He'd gone too far this time. He got a twelve-year sentence and had to pay £2.2 million in damages.

Anyway, I'd got back most of the equipment he'd taken on behalf of the Receivers, although the tractors and the lorry came back from Jack Harvey's Plant Hire minus their radios and various other extras.

Meanwhile, the Inland Revenue were hounding my mother and myself for the £18,000 that G Eustice & Son owed them, and we had were under a time deadline to raise the capital to secure the deal. In January and February we tried every lender we could think of.

We got turned down everywhere. The battle with Barclays had been very high profile and even though my view was that the bank had acted dishonourably and we had shown integrity, there was, I suppose, understandable nervousness from other lenders. Des even found us a loan shark to raise some of the initial tranche of money but I got cold feet and never did a deal with him, which I'm glad about.

I was over at Hay Farm in Wadebridge one night, seeing Martin, and we were talking about our businesses - he was involved with a supermarket that was in trouble at the time, and Adele and I were still trying to raise money to refinance the deal. It was that conversation with Martin that helped me face a difficult but perhaps necessary decision.

'You've got to let Tregotha go.' He said.

'The deal you have secured is a good one but it will still leave you with debt and probably difficulty servicing everything. Unless you secure the support of a lender to switch on the deal, you will lose the lot. What you need to do is to go to a lender with a proposal that they offer bridging finance to land the deal you have secured with Barclays and then sell at auction both Tregotha and Angarrack. That will raise the capital to ensure that you are left with the profitable part of the business at Trevaskis but with very low levels of debt.

It was obviously not easy to contemplate selling Tregotha, the farm where I had grown up and where things began. Martin knew that. Many times when we were children, my cousins came to Tregotha. He also knew that he was best placed to tell me. It was difficult but now was a time for hard-headed decisions.

'Adele's with Lloyds, isn't she? Why don't you talk to Richard Curnow? I've known him for years. I'll come along with you.'

Richard Curnow ran the Royal Cornwall Agricultural Association, but he also happened to be Adele's manager at Lloyds Bank in Truro.

So Adele and George and I went to see him with Martin. Richard Curnow seemed reasonably accepting of our proposals, although without Martin's connection to him we'd probably have got nowhere. What I didn't realise was that, at first, he thought we'd got no income to look forward to. In fact, we had a sizeable cauliflower harvest coming up, and when we told him about that he became quite hopeful. He told us that he'd want proper valuations and certified figures and, if we put a forward budget and plan together, he'd present the whole project to the right people at Lloyds and see what they said.

John Wakeham from Kivells, the auctioneers, had worked with Martin and Richard on another project for Lloyds, so Martin suggested we use him again.

We were by then within ten days of Barclays' deadline at the end of February. We had John Wakeham come down and I drove him around the farms. He and a colleague, an agricultural specialist, put together a plan, which involved an auction of Tregotha and the Angarrack Hill farmland. They worked on it until midnight to beat the clock.

Richard Curnow submitted it to Lloyds with his blessing and after a nail-biting delay, they said yes.

On March 1st 1996 the LPA Receivers were off the case, with no further claim on our livestock or deadstock.

The aftermath

With less land, my sons and I would have less to do but no more certainty than before. George had a project, his strawberries. Giles at this time had two jobs. In the daytime he helped me to run the Pick Your Own. At night - not every night - he managed a nightclub at the White Hart in Hayle called Strawberry Fields. He seemed happy enough, and he'd always had a talent for organising parties. But such a life didn't give him much scope for ambition, which is probably why he was lucky to be offered an opportunity away from Cornwall.

The way it happened was this. Serena was still an agronomist in Shropshire. Her then boyfriend, another agronomist called Nigel Gowling, was the man she was going to marry. One weekend in the spring of '96 they came down and brought Nigel's sister Sue with them. Sue ran a computer business in Hertfordshire called Abtec. She persuaded Giles to get involved in that. He was keen to try something different and I was sorry but at the same time pleased, because we felt that both the boys had suffered far too much from our problems ever since they came home from college. George was absorbed by a promising enterprise at Penryn but Giles was just treading water here.

So Giles had packed and was ready to leave for his new life in the Home Counties. It was May, 1996, and it would be his last night on the farm for a while.

Before first light I had to get him out of bed.

'I need you over at the cowshed to help,' I said. Rose, one of the South Devons, was having an agonising labour. So he came over too and helped while the vet did a Caesarian section. Giles never forgot the start of his last day here - partly because, at 4am, with the sun rising, the vet took a picture of Giles and me and Rose together.

When Tregotha and the Angarrack Hill land had to be sold, it hurt. It was spring then, April I think. The land felt like part of me, and I didn't want to see it farmed by anyone else.

The auction was well advertised and a lot of people expressed an interest. I got the inside track on what was going on from Mr Roust, who'd lived at Angarrack Hill Farmhouse since we sold it to keep John Bloor happy. The land there was being sold in three lots, and he said a gentleman had come to see it and said nothing would stand in his way of having it, and he was already a neighbour to it. I knew who that was; Michael Richards. I'd known him since we were both in Young Farmers.

There was interest in Tregotha Farm too, with the house of course. A friend called Bob Withers, a local fellow and a good businessman, had just sold a big plot of land in Truro to developers. He was keen to buy Tregotha and so was David Piccaver, from Piccaver's, the Lincolnshire growers who were already farming Upper Trevaskis.

The sale, conducted by John Wakeham of Kivell's, was held at the White Hart Hotel in Hayle. As usual with auctions there were a lot of people who were just snooping to see what the farms would make. But bidding was lively, and Michael Richards did buy the Angarrack Hill land.

David Piccaver and my friend Bob Withers competed for Tregotha Farm. They pushed it to a price well above its reserve and in the end, it was knocked down to Piccaver. He was going to grow vegetables on the land and live in the farmhouse.

Jersey Growers completed their purchase of Bezurrel and Lemin. What with that and the auction, the last £480,000 was cleared. I'd lost years of my work to Barclays; but at last I was out of their clutches.

George's strawberries were thriving under glass at Gabbons Nursery and that summer he would get £1.50 a punnet from Sainsbury's. He'd set us up to trade as Trevaskis Farm, and bought a small chiller lorry to take fruit to Sainsburys distribution centre. I rather liked driving it up-country.

When farmland is sold, its equipment and livestock are usually sold a few weeks later in a 'farm sale' held on the premises. This was urgent for us, because from now on we'd only have Trevaskis, which at 70 acres was less than one seventh of the land we'd held two years before. Adele had bought our animals and deadstock back by handing over that £330,000 but we wouldn't have room for so many cattle and we'd have to get rid of all the machinery we would no longer need.

The farm sale took place on a Saturday a week or two after Tregotha went. I was reminded of the last time we'd had such a thing here. It must have been in the early 1960s because it was soon after my father fell out with that Gwinear man, our enemy, over the piece of land. Dad sold his livestock at Drannack Mill Farm after that. Now I knew how he must have felt on that day. We would be selling nearly all of my beloved herd of pedigree South Devon cattle.

I had spent my working life building and refining the breed and judging, too, as a way to maintain standards, so I kept back a nucleus of about twenty South Devons to just make sure that I didn't lose the bloodlines of the herd. John Wakeham was an excellent Auctioneer but I wanted John Pappin, of the South Devon Herd Book Society, to sell my cows along with Keith Flemington from Bruton Knowles, the official Society auctioneer since 1976. I made the right choice because Keith achieved high prices from breeders from all over the British Isles.

John Wakeham auctioned the machinery and other deadstock. As I was walking down to the sale field, I saw two farmers coming up, a father and son. They'd been down looking at the tractors and balers and so on. The son was saying to the father, "What a load of old rubbish that is.' I felt sad, because we'd never wasted money on flashy bells and whistles but always got whatever would work best for the job I wanted it to do.

Tregotha Farm, of course, was vacated before the sale. Alan Cook had to leave the house he'd occupied for many years, but he found another place in the village. My mother went to live with my sister and brother-in-law, Catherine and Adrian, at Mount Pleasant Farm. Her furniture and most of her possessions were carried off to Lane's Storage and Removals at Truro. That turned out to be a drain on our resources but at least thanks to the good price the farm sale had raised there was enough to pay for it in Adele's bank account.

The sale day was traumatic for me. I broke down when it was over. And yet for the first time in ages we were significantly in credit, with a familiar roof over our head and the Pick Your Own and the restaurant. When you woke up on a sunny summer morning you felt free. It was over.

I was keen to settle up all with all the good people who had bills outstanding, like Joanne Richards and many others. The law decreed that the Revenue would get their money first, but suppliers who'd supported me through the worst times stayed at the top of my personal list. Those further down were the ones who'd put the boot in when I was at a low ebb.

At first, I had to tell all of them to be patient and hold on and wait for me to recover and get back on my feet. And those people all got paid the money that they were owed.

The one creditor that never got a bean was Gwinear and District Farmers. I'd been their President. I'd been their Vice

Chairman. I'd been on their committee for 20 years plus. When I went bankrupt I still owed them about £10,000, because I was their largest customer and was loyal to them. My grandfather had been a founder member of Gwinear and District Farmers and he'd put his own money in to help when they were in trouble during the difficult 1930s. So of course I supported them.

As G & G Eustice, after the bankruptcy, our family tried to negotiate an arrangement to pay them in full, a certain amount per month over and above whatever we owed them for our purchases. It might take a while but we'd be back in credit with them in two or three years. They were having none of it. They wanted us to put a hefty sum onto our slate and top it up as we spent money with them. Uncle Derrick was on their committee and dissented; he told the others 'If you're not careful, you'll get nothing.'

Sadly for them, he was right.

I found another supplier easily enough, through a friend on the Board of Cornwall Farmers. They gave us a monthly account for our farming needs and for horticulture we bought from Avoncrop at Bristol. George used to spend quite a lot with them because his strawberry enterprise was already up and running with all the greenhouses in full production.

Giles had begun a new life; George was engaged at Penryn; and the faithful men who had worked with me for so long had all left to do other things because we could no longer afford to pay them. It wasn't fair for them to stay in a business where there was little future.

That winter John Eddy, our driver, had gone to Winchester Bulbs to work. He went there and became a foreman and ganger.

Anthony Mitchell had been with me 25 years. He'd said to me one day, 'What is going to happen?'

'Well, I don't know Anthony, I'm not too sure.'

'I'm asking because I've been offered another job.'

'Who's that with then?'

'Dennis Archdale.' Dennis farmed Roseworthy, a big place neighbouring Trevaskis Farm. He grew vegetables and sugar beet, and he'd offered Anthony a job because he knew the troubles that I was suffering.

'You go, Anthony,' I said, 'You couldn't work for a better man. You'd better not stay here because I don't know what is going to happen to us at all. You won't regret getting a job there with Dennis Archdale.' I was sad to see him go but relieved that he had a good job.

Colin Morris had worked with Uncle Derek at Bezurrel and for me there, too. Dennis Archdale took him on. In the end the only one left was Alan Cook. He didn't want to leave because of the cattle, who were back at Tregotha when all this happened.

For some months Alan Cook came to Trevaskis to work but with so few cows, he had to get involved with the fruit growing business part-time and that wasn't really what he wanted. Eventually he left to work with more livestock than we had.

In July of 1996 I received a demand for about £20,000 from a firm of factors. They were collecting payment for Des's services as a consultant. Since factoring works as it does, Des would almost certainly have got most of the money out of them months ago, having somehow persuaded them that I was a good risk.

The factors were threatening court proceedings. I got Des to turn up at court to ask, as the original creditor, for my hearing to be postponed for a few months, to give me time to pay. It was an unusual situation but debts rarely get written off, I'd still have to pay in the end. I had letters from Bond Pearce representing Barclays, letters from my accountants, letters from the factors and the Inland Revenue. My mother was pursued by the Revenue for a long time. We did not succeed in reaching a settlement for her until 1997, when she was 80.

George was corresponding with all these people; I was too badly damaged by the whole experience. There was a whole bundle of last straws here and the camel's back was sagging like a hammock. Since I couldn't pay much of what I owed I visited an insolvency practitioner, expecting to be advised of some way around the problem.

I laid my case before this man. He listened. He nodded. He took notes, made a list of creditors and amounts. He was silent for a moment. Then raised his eyebrows at me, leaned back in his chair and said

'There's only one way out Mr Eustice. You have to declare bankruptcy.'

I hadn't expected to become bankrupt in the year of my fiftieth birthday and I was devastated. For me, it was the final humiliation.

I went bankrupt at a court hearing in Truro in the late summer of 1996; a demeaning day for me.

Because I was bankrupt, any money I earned, above a subsistence amount, had to go to my creditors. The livestock and deadstock, the farm shop and restaurant, and most of the land at Trevaskis were Adele's property; I could contribute very little, financially. I was out of it, and I felt that I was quite a failure in many ways, because I now had to step back. I was still advising everyone within the business, but I could no longer take any part in it.

Nor, apparently, was I any longer a fit person to represent the Royal Cornwall Show. Eustices had been stewards and committee members since I was born if not before, but when it came to making that decision, I was the last to know. I got no letter of apology, explanation or word of gratitude for past help. In '97 my Steward's badge and paperwork didn't turn up, and not until I arrived for a committee meeting was I told I'd been blackballed. A year or two later the Royal Cornwall Committee took a table and ate dinner at the restaurant. There and then they asked Hugh Lello to ask me if I'd come back. It was mean of them to hide behind him and he was embarrassed. I told them, in short, to get lost.

1996 did bring some happiness too. In September, Serena was married in Gwinear Church, a beautiful ancient place. She has always loved horses so she was carried in a horse-drawn carriage from the church to Trevaskis, where a marquee had been set up in front of the restaurant. We decorated it with hops I'd brought down from Worcester in the chiller lorry, we did all the catering ourselves and Giles organised the music. Besides celebrating the union of Serena and Nigel, we wanted to express our gratitude to everyone who'd helped us in our hard times. Friends of ours came down from Norfolk, Serena's college friends arrived from all over, and we had a lovely day.

Treading the bottom

For two or three years I felt almost hopeful again. The restaurant was doing well, but then it always did. Trevaskis Farm was fine. We had a lorry and we could buy straw from a neighbour for our cattle, and rent grazing land from him. So although we had a smaller herd it was well cared for. George bought some big poly-tunnels from Portugal at a bargain price. We put them on Trevaskis and he was able to supply about a tenth of the British market by harvesting first at Penryn, then at Trevaskis. Because of the three-year rotation he'd always have early strawberries to sell.

Serena and Nigel were making big changes in their own lives. For one thing, in 1998 Serena was expecting our first grandchild, Charlie. For another, she was in her final year of training as a solicitor.

The few days she had spent observing events at the High Court hearing in Bristol, plus the agricultural expertise she'd got, had convinced her that a farmer like me would always be hard pressed to argue his case without professional help from somebody who understood his business. She'd spotted a niche market that was ill-served by most barristers. Even Siobhan Ward, who had seemed pretty good until she dropped us, had lacked specialist experience of agriculture. Serena had a good degree already, and a day job, so began by taking a law conversion course at evening classes. She then took a legal practice course and, after Charlie was born, she would spend at least a year working in a solicitor's office to get practical experience and qualify.

She and Nigel were still in Shropshire. The two years after Charlie's birth she devoted to three main activities – work, study and child care. Her practical experience was gained at

Burges Salmon, so she and Nigel moved to Tetbury in Gloucestershire, thirty miles from Bristol. She had to drive to Bristol every morning after getting Charlie dressed and fed and ferrying him to the childminder. She had demands on her time every hour of every day. I went up there for a while as baby-sitter and rather enjoyed myself fixing up their garden.

Adele and I travelled about every summer to the country shows. We had a tent from which we sold fruit and vegetables and thanks to George's greenhouses at Penryn, strawberries and cream from a refrigerated trailer.

We didn't see the first signs of another downturn in our affairs until the price of strawberries began to fall. George had benefited, in 1997, from being the first in the market. But it didn't take long for other growers to catch on. In the spring of '99, with costs of production rising and the price paid by Sainsburys exactly half what he'd got when he started, he knew we'd need to diversify again. He came up with the brilliant idea of a Maize Maze (which is exactly what you think it is) at Trevaskis in time for the total eclipse in August of '99. I seem to have been busy all summer with that, driving to Southampton to help the designer, and then setting it up. On the day it attracted many people, made money and looked absolutely spectacular. We erected a few little bridges over the maize, and we stood on one of those to watch the moon hide the sun through special glasses. And, I was asked to judge at the Royal of England Show again that year, which lifted my spirits considerably.

In the autumn of the Millennium year, we planted trees. I'd originally bought them for Bezurrel, where we needed to replace trees lost to Dutch Elm disease. Instead we put them in at Trevaskis.

Giles was enjoying his new life and George was getting involved in politics. He stood in 1999 as a Member of the European

Parliament. My role in that was hammering VOTE EUSTICE placards into place. I put up signs along what felt like every country road in the South West. Despite my efforts George didn't get in, but he remained passionate about saving the pound sterling at a time when there was a clamour to join the Eurozone. He was even offered a job in London by Business for Sterling.

Once she qualified, Serena was engaged as a full-time solicitor by Burges Salmon. So she had a decent income, which was a relief because as soon as she got the job, Nigel almost immediately quit his, to study full-time for a year and become a barrister.

Unfortunately, none of these advances could compensate entirely for the rising cost of producing strawberries and the declining price they could achieve. George was beginning to look seriously for a life beyond farming. I came into the office one day and he was sitting there, musing, staring out of the window. On the screen in front of him was a spreadsheet: the figures for the strawberries. His margins were so low now, because of the glut in the market and the rising price of fuel and other necessities, that pretty soon he wouldn't be making enough to break even. Suddenly he looked across and spoke to me.

'I think I should look for another job,' he said.

I'd seen it coming. Our small acreage at Trevaskis wasn't paying its way either, and in 2000 Adele and I were seeing real trouble ahead. We'd gone into the red again and we knew what the consequences might ultimately be.

'That's fine George. You have a go at something else. If you ever want to work with us again - your mother and I will keep this going and if you ever want to come back it will be here for you to take on.'

He told me I could take the Penryn enterprise over if I wanted to; it was easy to run. But I didn't want the effort of growing excellent crops only to have supermarkets pay derisory sums that didn't cover costs.

'Thanks for the offer, George,' I said 'but if Sainsburys want early strawberries they can grow their own, as far as I'm concerned.'

So we dismantled the equipment, sold the machinery, and George took the job with Business for Sterling, which eventually became a full-time career in politics. Our trial, horrible as it was, had made both George and Serena aware of the possibilities open to them as individuals. They'd recognised an unspoken need. Farmers need expert professionals to represent them – people who really understand their struggles.

-

When George set off on a path to a different life, Adele and I had tough decisions to make. I had only recently been discharged from bankruptcy and once again demands were descending on us from all sides. This time, we weren't going to be anybody's punchbag.

We took advice from estate agents and decided to sell our home. We would market Trevaskis Farmhouse, a field and Mother's barn conversion as one lot. Adele would be left with an income from the shop, restaurant and Pick Your own, and she'd still own our car park and twenty acres of Trenawin above the railway line. With the proceeds of the farmhouse sale, and all debts cleared, we'd be able to build ourselves a house near the restaurant.

There was one flaw in this excellent, stress-reducing plan. If we completed the sale of Trevaskis Farmhouse and everything else before we got planning permission to build, we'd have nowhere to live. I consulted the planners to find out what they wanted from us, had plans drawn up and put our case. We had to live here, to be able to look after the livestock and crops and protect the restaurant. You couldn't just lock up and leave it all exposed to thieves, squatters or arsonists, so we needed at the very least to have permission for a new house before we sold the old one.

We put the application before West Penwith Council's Planning Committee and it was turned down. They took the view that because we had a house and were selling it, we did not deserve to have another one.

No buyer appeared. Our property was still up for sale, so we just got on with our lives. I planted trees. I went ferreting. I went off judging up and down the country. Adele was tipped off about a thief among the restaurant staff, took her to court and the woman was fined. She'd stolen about ten thousand pounds by then. Adele was devastated, because she had always trusted her.

So that was a nasty life lesson. In other respects, we were treading water and living with anxiety. Our home of over thirty years was on the market. My mother was still living in the converted cottage next door and when we sold up, she'd have to go somewhere. The restaurant was doing well but the small amount of farmland we had was not making money all year round. I'd sold the strawberries-and-cream trailer; too much hassle.

Another faithful dog died.

We had no idea what people might pay for what we'd achieved, so in despair we put our livelihood, as well as our home, up for sale: the Trevaskis farmhouse, all the land, the conversion that my mother lived in, the restaurant and farm shop and the Pick Your own. At the very least, we would learn what people would pay.

We had all sorts of people traipsing about, viewing. Only one couple, from Ireland, were seriously prepared to buy the whole lot. They loved Cornwall, they looked forward to farming in a place like this, but farming was all they knew. These days, in this country, farmers are chasing a huge and fickle market. They need business competence, customer focus and a perpetual readiness to learn and diversify. Those two rightly felt that the retail and restaurant side of it was going to be too much for them. They'd make us an offer, but they'd want us to remain as managers. We thought long and hard about that and remained uncertain until the day they put an offer on the table. That was the end of that. We couldn't sell for so little.

All around us, farmland and houses were being bought and sold and rented out. David Piccaver had had Tregotha for a few years; other people farmed it until finally the land ended up with Jersey Growers and Tregotha farmhouse was sold to a very nice couple called Mr and Mrs Laws, who converted the outbuildings to holiday lets.

Around this time we were approached by Railtrack, which then owned the track and most of the stations in Britain. After a run of horrific accidents on level crossings, they were looking to close the most dangerous ones. There were two of those near us, and one was where the main railway line bisected Trevaskis. If they could construct a new road across our Trenawen land, they told us, they could shut both the dangerous crossings. There would be compensation. We were quite keen, because we'd have money to re-shape the business again. So although having a road there would be inconvenient in some ways, it would be a potential source of capital. I didn't object, although I had to explain this new development to the solicitor who would handle the sale of Trevaskis; the likelihood that there might be a new road might affect a decision to buy, and we were anxious to sell the house so that West Penwith Council would have to concede that we needed a new one.

Our buyers were not deterred, and in the February of 2000, we exchanged contracts on Trevaskis farmhouse and mother's cottage as well. We obviously had to be out before completion, so we had to re-apply for planning permission right away, since we had nowhere to go. We decided that while the house was built we'd live in a caravan next to the car park.

Once again the Cornwall Council Planning Committee at Penzance considered our application. We had the support of several of its members. We submitted letters from our bank manager and our MP. How could we fail?

The officers of West Penwith council recommended refusal, and they'd managed to get the County Land Agent on their side. Most of the planners concurred with them. One of those who didn't, who was particularly frustrated at the result rang me up and said he was disgusted, because they must have known they would leave Adele and me, and my 83-year-old mother, homeless.

'If it was up to that bunch, St Michael's Mount wouldn't have got built.'

He said he'd make an appointment for me to see the Chief Planning Officer to get permission for a caravan on the site.

'Don't do that,' I said. 'It's asking for trouble. They refuse everything I ask them for. I'm going to put one up anyway.'

I think it was July when the new owners of Trevaskis (old friends of ours) finally moved into it. A woman friend of theirs came down from Oxfordshire and bought mother's cottage.

Now that moving day was in sight, Adele and I were paralysed by misery. We couldn't face it. Our children saved us, as they always would. George and Giles came down the weekend before completion, boxed everything up, and took the furniture and goods and chattels down to Adele's father's house at St Buryan, and her sister Charmaine's house.

I bought the cheapest caravan I could find in reasonable condition for £300. I looked covetously at an upmarket one, but we agreed that the Planners couldn't hold out forever and we wouldn't live in it for more than a year, so the extra expense would be pointless. We had a big kitchen, at the restaurant. All we needed was a bed, somewhere to keep clean, room for our clothes and bedlinen and the dog, and a table to do the accounts on.

We parked our bijou home well away from the road, maybe 200 feet from the restaurant, where it could be supplied with running water and electricity. We took only the bare necessities with us from Trevaskis but it still felt like living in a cupboard. It kept us dry, but the walls were thin fibreglass and not well insulated from heat, cold or sound (out or in). My mother was in hospital for a few months when the houses were sold, and when she recovered she had to go back to Catherine and Adrian's to live.

We launched a petition to the Planning Committee and collected about 5,000 signatures from restaurant customers that summer.

I looked for ways to make money. I wanted to grow soft fruit in tunnels and experiment with tabletop growing - you erect long lines of narrow waist-high troughs, grow the fruit in peat-based compost in there, and install an automatic irrigation system. The paths between the lines are wide enough for picking and spraying.

I had polytunnels, but in the wrong place. We had to move our old ones away from the field by Trevaskis and up towards the restaurant - a very difficult job, because thick polythene, in bulk, is even heavier than you'd think, and unwieldy, and access wasn't simple. Whichever way you looked at it, you had to get down a hill, under a bridge and up a hill. Railtrack hadn't done anything about the new road yet.

Access over our land had been an off and on issue for years. At one time, farm vehicles avoiding the low bridge used to cross the railway line further north - but that came to an end when a train smashed into a tractor in the 1960s. A crowd of us were out in the fields working and we all looked up when we heard the bang. A terrible accident and the tractor driver was killed.

However we expected Railtrack to come back to us soon and say they were ready to pay me £40,000 in compensation, remove the crossing and build a new road; so I erected a shed for the livestock and created a new yard area above the railway line.

I'd observed that people were getting interested in organic produce. They wanted to grow their own but didn't know how. So by leafleting at garden centres, I set myself up as a kitchen garden consultant; I'd install and explain a garden if that's what was wanted, or I'd do that and then maintain it. I enjoyed doing that and found it easily fitted around my work on the Pick-Your-Own. My very first customer was Roger Thomas down at the Old Vicarage in St Erith, and his enthusiasm was terrifically encouraging. From then on there was no stopping me - I established or improved kitchen gardens from Truro to Land's End. I gave it up after a couple of years because the Pick Your Own business was thriving and needed a lot more time, but really I could have made a career out of kitchen gardens up and down the country. I enjoyed the travel and I met a lot of good people. I always took pictures of what I'd done, and notes on why I'd done it, and they came in useful when I began teaching an organic gardening evening class at Cornwall College. It's gratifying, passing on what you've learned, and it keeps you on your toes as well. I was even invited to give a talk at the Eden

Project, where they were interested in the way we grew our soft fruit at Trevaskis.

I fully expected to enjoy judging for the South Devon Herd Book Society again. Some of us set off and travelled up and down the country like the year before, but we had to call the whole thing off before we made our final farm visit. 2001 was the Plague Year, the nightmare time of foot and mouth in cattle, when restrictions were in place throughout Britain and Ireland and millions of animals, the vast majority perfectly healthy, were destroyed, on the firebreak principle.

Piecing our life back together

For the first five years of the twenty-first century I made a living out of various enterprises, while Adele's restaurant steadily did better and better. For probably the first time in my working life, I remained entirely debt-free. It's true that until I took on Bezurrel, I hadn't worried about the overdraft. I had known it was there, but then an overdraft had probably supported G Eustice & Son since I left school, if not before. I'd never felt fearful before 1993 because our debt was manageable and the boys would inherit expertise and land. Had I been living in a fool's paradise? Probably, but fear is what ruins lives, not optimism.

After Bloor and his friends moved in on me, my anxiety level had been sky high for two or three years. Adele and the boys were the same. Now, the only thing wearing us down was West Penwith Council, with our enemy on it. In fact he had been Dad's enemy, still apparently bearing a grudge against all Eustice men half a century after the feud began and fourteen years after Dad died.

We were trapped in our tiny caravan, unable to build. The council told us to remove the caravan from the land and sent an enforcement notice, which would be followed by bailiffs. We didn't panic; we'd been there, done it all – but uncertainty is unsettling, so we decided that professional help was required. We turned to Burges Salmon for advice, and also engaged Bruton Knowles to put our case for building. But they didn't achieve a stay of execution on the enforcement notice and when we got a second caravan and parked it next to ours, the flow of angry orders from the council intensified. The fact was, my mother had rung me one evening and announced that she was ready to come back to live here. She had decided not to live with Catherine any more, but with us; and nobody argued with my mother. So we got a second caravan and she moved in.

We hadn't asked for this situation. We didn't like it. What the council were doing felt like persecution. My anxiety level was going up again, and I knew Adele was stressed although she somehow faced the public with a smile in spite of our living conditions.

One weekend, a couple I'd never seen before went for tea to the restaurant after they'd had their fruit weighed, as most of the pick-your-own crowd did. They'd seen the caravans on the grass beside the car park, and read the petition, and the man asked me what was going on.

'We're being evicted by the council. We don't want to be in those caravans but they won't let us build a house here to run our business from.'

'What's their objection?'

'Well at first they said we already had a house. We did, we had Trevaskis farmhouse down there but we had to sell it. So now they say we can find somewhere in the village. But we need to be on site - we've got animals here.'

I was careful about my answers because I was suspicious of everyone by then; I wasn't sure who he was or what his intentions were. But he told me that he'd got quite a lot of experience with planning applications and he seemed to understand our position at once. He wrote 'Geoff Hill' and his telephone number on a piece of paper and told me to call if I needed any help. He seemed a good sort so I thanked him but didn't think much about it because we'd already engaged advisors.

But Bruton Knowles, and our solicitors, still seemed half asleep, and I didn't know what to do because we were at imminent risk of being evicted from our own land by West Penwith Council.

So I decided to ring this Geoff Hill who'd taken an interest but I'd lost the piece of paper. I had to try to remember what he'd said. I rang friends; I knew he came from a village near Truro and eventually I tracked him down.

I invited him down for a chat and he was very helpful indeed. He talked over the whole problem and found the positives. One key fact (which nobody else had even asked about) was that I still held an agricultural holding number for the land. That's a bit like a passport specific to the place. It smoothes a farmer's passage through the paperwork on everything from moving cattle to applying for grants or permits.

Geoff told us to put up a fence and make a garden. We needed the caravans to look like permanent structures, obviously inhabited and a deterrent to anyone thinking of robbing the restaurant or otherwise doing harm. We could even put in swings and slides for our grandchildren. I made a garden that looked pretty, tidy, and permanent, as if the caravan was a home we cared about.

We still had to fight the enforcement notice. Serena and Nigel, as well as Geoff Hill and his wife, went to Penzance to do exactly that, and won.

We'd defeated them, and rested for a while before going into battle again. We would re-submit our planning application for a house when we were ready.

I'd look up, sometimes, of an evening, when lorries passed as I worked in my garden. They'd be driving to the pack house with their day's load of caulis. These days all the farms in Gwinear Parish and surrounding parishes sent cauliflowers to one of two big pack houses, one at Higher Trevaskis near us, and another at Leedstown.

The supermarkets have changed farming for good. The new system is efficient and saves fuel but it means that farmers are dealing with faceless organisations rather than knowing their wholesalers personally. Unless they bite the bullet and sell direct to consumers, they have no control over prices or variety; everything is dictated by the supermarkets. I don't envy them. I'd always enjoyed my trips up country to the markets and I learned a lot from people I met, too.

Both my sons have, by a twist of fate, managed to be diverted into different walks of life. In many ways I am glad of that. Most of the farmers' sons in Gwinear Parish and many of the other parishes are still around, driving their own tractors and machinery but reliant on their contracts with the pack houses. They are important cogs in a big retail machine but they are not well paid and are in no position to negotiate anything better.

When I was a boy there were regular livestock markets at Camborne, Redruth, Penzance and Helston. These days there is just one left, at Truro. And again, it is efficient but prices are far beyond control of the farming community.

Caravan or not, I was probably having a better time of it in the early 2000s than a lot of farmers. I had at least managed to keep control of my own small patch, where I was growing my fruit and vegetables to sell through our farm shop. And we had the livestock. School tours were coming round Trevaskis now and I introduced a few sheep - a rare breed, Greyface Dartmoors. I was surprised to find, when I looked back through their history, that my grandfather had been one of the first Flock Book members back in the very early 1930s at Tregotha. Visitors were fascinated by the sheep, which are more cream than grey, with curly-haired faces and massive thick woolly fleeces in winter.

My Uncle Derrick, who had taught me so much about pig-keeping and struggled beside me to keep all the family farms together, had moved to Hayle. He came one summer's day in the early 2000s to pick gooseberries and mentioned in passing that he'd been diagnosed with cancer. I was shocked, but 'these days' I reassured him 'a lot can be done.'

Adele and I were sad, and shaken, but he didn't seem ill and was getting treatment.

Both of us were working hard at the time. We'd had a very good butcher working for us for several years who turned out to have been helping not just us, but himself. He was walking off with money from the till. I had to tell him to leave, and after that I did the butchery myself in the evenings. I'd started to build up the British Lops again, and was fattening them on waste bakery from the restaurant. Big mistake. Pigs fed on sticky buns get obese. Joanne Richards, at JV Richards, who used to do our slaughtering, told me she couldn't use the carcasses. Butchers wouldn't take them because they were more fat than pork.

So I wasn't sure how to cope with the fat pigs I had, and I asked a former butcher; Robin, in fact, who'd chased the thieves with Giles that time. He'd closed his shop a few years ago, but he said

'I've still got all the gear at home. I'll bring it up to you one day and show you how to make sausages and hog's pudding and use up all the surplus fat.'

He came and showed me what to do, and although he already had a part-time job I offered him another one. He agreed, and came to us two or three times a week to make sausages and do our butchering. I'd been looking after that side of the farm shop for a while by then, but an inspector from the council told me I needed to display a certificate of competence. Fair enough – the shop was doing well and nobody had ever asked me for a certificate, but I had to get it, so I went up to London (a six-hour journey, and six hours back) to do a course, three Tuesdays in a row. The certificate was put in a frame and hung in the shop. I suppose the man from the council chalked that up as a victory. Eustices 1, West Penwith 2.

Our farm shop had begun a stall in a shed, selling fruit and vegetables to passing tourists and families taking a day out to pick their own fruit. Now that we had a purpose-built shop, a fresh meat section, and baked goods, we were a fully fledged retail outlet and therefore supposed to stay open all year round. But we were on an unclassified road in a county that relied on summer visitors and there was very little passing trade in winter, so we applied to West Penwith Council for permission to close the shop between November and April.

Given what we knew of their attitude to us, we were unsurprised when they refused. They could not deny that we would lose money by staying open. We could close, they said, as long as we shut the restaurant as well. That wasn't going to happen since we got an income from the restaurant all year round and Christmas lunches at Trevaskis were already an institution. Many families came every single year.

We gritted our teeth and decided to invest in the farm shop so that people would find a reason to go out of their way to come in all weathers and spend money there.

Then Ben died; my collie who had been inseparable from me all his life. We had to bury him near the caravans. It was inexpressibly sad.

You can survive in a small immobile caravan, but that's about all you can do. You can pretend things are normal but you really can't *live*. There's never enough room. And at key times – the festivals, the weddings, the dog dying – you're forced to face the abnormality and limitations of your situation head on.

Christmas was like that. It was an event even more divorced from daily life than usual, but in a good way. Afterwards, we returned to the caravan trying to avoid thinking about all our future uncertainties. The first year, my mother went to Adrian and Catherine at Porthtowan, but we were facing a couple of cold days on our own because George, Serena and Giles were all away working upcountry. Happily Giles found a house to rent on Helford River and we all gathered there, had a lovely time and drank toasts to a better life. The following year we all spent Christmas at Giles's house in Hertfordshire. That time my mother came too. Unfortunately she was taken ill and had to be admitted to a hospital, so I had to stay at Giles's until she was well enough to bring home. And so it went on, as another, and another, and yet another Christmas rolled around. We had underestimated how much trouble local councillors can cause.

Row upon row of cauliflowers are paradise for rabbits and, around 2003, I had a running battle on. I needed another dog and I rather fancied having a fast one, bred for the chase. It had to be a lurcher. I looked at some in Torquay and others in Plymouth, and a puppy caught my eye from several in a litter still too young to remove from their mother. I had to judge South Devons at the Honiton Show in ten days' time, though, so the breeder said I could pick him up then. I did, and brought him home on an extremely hot August day in 2003. Rough-haired, affectionate, and white all over with black markings, Jack grew big, leggy and fast, and was just the sort of dog that I wanted. I had hours of fun with him keeping the rabbits down off the vegetables at Trevaskis.

The worst thing that happened in 2004 was Uncle Derrick's death in January. He'd been diagnosed quite late I think and one day last autumn at Trevaskis, he'd told me there was nothing further that the doctors could do.

After that miserable start, and the funeral, things slowly picked up. We re-submitted our plans for a house. Geoffrey Curnow, the County Land Agent who'd opposed us before, said his piece. On no evidence whatsoever, West Penwith decided that we were simply trying to make a quick buck by adding value to the site. If we got permission, they said, we could build the house next to the business and sell the whole large site as a going concern. It was agricultural land and if we built a house we'd set a precedent. We didn't even need a house but could live in the village.

We had heard most of this before, but they were becoming more hostile with time. To hear their case you'd think we'd asked permission to tarmac the whole place and erect a tower block and a casino. They turned us down flat.

With help from Geoff Hill we decided to appeal. The hearing took place at Cornwall Council's offices in Penzance. Several of our customers came to speak on our behalf. Serena and Nigel arrived and helped a lot. The Cornwall Council Inspector, who knew Trevaskis, was unconvinced by West Penwith and sympathetic to us. We should be able to erect a house on the site, he said, but – to reassure our local councillors that we weren't property developers– we'd have to live in the caravans for three years first.

We were delighted. We didn't look forward to three more years in the fibreglass cupboard, but what a relief it is to know that the future will be better. Also, we'd have lots of time to do the fun part of housebuilding, the thinking and choosing and imagining, before the groundwork started and the cement truck made a habit of getting in the way.

Thanks to Chancellor Brown's decision that we shouldn't join the Euro after all, Business for Sterling was winding down and no longer needed its Campaign Director. George had done a good job there so off he went to Conservative Central Office and worked for Michael Howard.

Serena had left Burges Salmon a couple of years before to be a solicitor at MFG in Worcester. She'd recently been promoted to associate partner there and had begun to train as a barrister. She and Nigel had a second son and they lived at Ross-on-Wye.

In 2004 the firm Giles worked for were finding competition tough and there was talk of laying people off. Giles had to think what he really wanted to do with his life. The draw of Cornwall was too much, I think. He rented a cottage in a village near us and came back to work at Trevaskis Farm.

Adele and I were all smiles. What a relief it was; after eight years away, he'd returned at just the moment when we knew we needed someone to take the business forward. Trevaskis Farm Limited was a lot of work, especially now that we'd expanded it again. We were already in our late fifties and we'd been wondering if we really would have to sell up in the next few years, and allow West Penwith to say *Told You So*.

The three-year moratorium on building gave us plenty of time to find a design for the house we wanted. We looked at timber-frame options and had some plans drawn up, but the result wouldn't look right here. We then found a big company called Pottons, visited their timber-frame show houses in Cambridgeshire, and decided to have one of those.

I was still expecting compensation for the land at Trenawin when the man from Railtrack told me they might not be able to get planning permission for the road after all. Julie (the lady from Oxfordshire who now owned my mother's old cottage) and the couple in our old house at Trevaskis had all raised strong objections.

I needed Railtrack's compensation to build the business. I went down to see Julie and she confirmed that they didn't want the road coming through there. They'd all known it could happen because it had been clearly understood when they bought the farm and the cottage, but they'd bought anyhow, gambling that they could oppose it and win. I said:

'If I'd known that, I wouldn't have factored the road and the compensation into all our plans for the past four years.'

So she said 'What's it worth to you?'

'To give them planning permission? I was going to have £40,000 off them.'

She said 'I'll buy that land for forty thousand.'

We shook hands on it.

So, when Railtrack came back to me the next week I said

'I've sold it; it's out of my hands now.'

'When? This is a bit sudden.'

'I've come to an arrangement with the buyer.'

'Well if there's nothing signed you can change it.'

'No, I've done the deal,' I said. 'I don't go back on my word.' Julie paid me, and I transferred the Trenawin land to her; it wasn't my problem any more.

When Giles came back he was still knowledgeable about growing crops but he knew very little about the restaurant because it had always been the responsibility of Adele and Charmaine. Neither of the boys had ever worked there. As soon as they left school they were out on the land. But Giles, in his own home in Hertfordshire, had become a good cook and he spent most of his time in the kitchens with Adele.

He'd always liked foreign food and foreign cooking, and he got more and more absorbed by the restaurant. Adele showed him how the kitchen and restaurant worked together. Then he spent time finding out about the livestock, the pick your own and the crops, and pretty soon he was fully involved, more so than ever before. Also in 2005 he was smitten with a new girlfriend, a local girl, Hannah.

Serena had passed her Bar exams, and we went to Temple Inn to see her admitted. She would specialise in agricultural litigation, as she had done as a solicitor. George was there of course. That year there had been an election, and Michael Howard, who had been Leader, resigned when the Conservatives lost to Labour again. David Cameron became Leader of the Opposition and asked George to work for him, which he did.

A new day dawns, with problems of a different sort

In 2006 we were getting closer to the time when we could build our house, and Giles decided it was time to upgrade the restaurant. He put together everything he'd learned when he was up in Hertfordshire, and everything he knew about catering, and came up with an ambitious plan to double the size of the kitchens and the restaurant and broaden its market.

So we shut the restaurant and a cheerful bunch of men in hard hats and high-viz jackets turned up every morning. The contractors added a whole new building, and Kevin Tregunna, Giles's cousin from Truro, did a lovely job on the interior. By the time all the workers left you couldn't recognise the place. I was away some of the time anyway because I went to Hong Kong for the Rugby Sevens. My trip was a sixtieth birthday present from Serena, George and Giles. I got on the plane wondering who I was going to talk to for the next few days, but as soon as I landed I spotted another farmer. I fell in with him and his wife. Their son was in Hong Kong playing for Wales, and we had a great time together.

Back home, Jack had a companion. A little lost terrier cross had been brought into the restaurant. Adele, who has a very soft heart, took her from the arms of the lady who found her and said we'd look after her until she was claimed. We rang around the RSPCA, Radio Cornwall, the police, everywhere but she must have been abandoned or lost for a long time because you could see her ribs, under her coat, and she wolfed every meal we put in front of her. We kept her safe and after a few days, if a claimant had turned up we'd certainly have given them the third degree. She was quite a little character. So I took her to the vet, got her microchipped, and she had a home. We called her Jilly, to go with Jack. At first, she had to be kept away from children; she was scared and aggressive. You never know what rescued animals have been through. But she settled and became an affectionate little dog.

We had far fewer cattle now. Thirty of my South Devons had to be sold in 2005 because the landowner I rented their fields from had decided to grow vegetables there. I was pleased when Julian Collins bought them. He was an old friend of Uncle Derrick's who had lost all his British Lops because of foot and mouth in 2001. Julian's pigs had been healthy, but were officially compromised by a remote possibility of contact; it is a highly infectious disease and they were condemned for that reason. He decided to keep cattle this time, and I knew they would be well cared for.

I kept only six or eight South Devons, to maintain the bloodline, and saw the rest off saying 'Look after them, now. I might be back for them one day.' Julian could see I was unhappy to see them go and promised to give me first refusal if he ever decided to retire.

When the restaurant renovation was complete, Giles worked there full-time. The restaurant and shop together were an instant market for all the strawberries and vegetables we could grow and I even had to supplement supplies with produce from Bristol Market. I have always liked driving around England because travel distracts you from worries, and there have been times in my life when that was necessary. Also, after year upon year in the caravan where Adele had to do her accounts on a tiny formica table every night, we both needed occasional solitude.

We hired a van at first, and then bought a new pickup to which I added a trailer. It turned out to be cheaper to buy from the market than to grow everything. We had an excellent Polish fellow called Marius working on the farm with us; a good all-rounder who would turn his hand to anything. We decided to expand the pick-your-own and the polytunnel growing because both, in different ways, supported the restaurant. So did our new organic kitchen garden near the restaurant. We installed two of the extra polytunnels we'd bought and laid out south-facing raised beds for planting in front of them. There was even a pond. We surrounded the whole thing with picket fence and used it as a way to demonstrate how to grow almost anything organically: peaches, apricots, figs, grapes, blueberries – by carefully training delicate crops against walls, and growing salad crops and early potatoes in tunnels, you can add a lot of variety to your diet.

That was in 2006, and ten years later it's still thriving, with school groups and organic growing courses. We had more than one fantastic Polish worker. Maybe they succeeded so well here because they felt really involved. They could see this was a family business and that was the kind of background they came from. All the growers in the area were getting their vegetables planted and harvested by foreign labour by then. As we'd found years ago, it was nigh on impossible to find reliable local people to do that work.

At last, in 2007 we were awarded planning permission for our new house and the ground could be cleared. Adele and I were excited and impatient– and on site. We could see progress every day, and I can hardly describe the difference that made. We'd lived in a space about 110 feet square for seven years now and would soon be moving into something about 25 times bigger. No more shivering in winter and boiling in summer; no more huddling in one room; and we'd have proper showers and proper toilets and a big garden. It was everything we wanted.

In November 2008, we were looking forward to our first Christmas in the house. We had a tractor that needed converting to four-wheel drive, so I drove it onto a trailer and hauled it up to North Wales to be converted, and in January I went back with the trailer to collect it. I broke the journey back at Serena's in Ross-on-Wye and saw all three (yes, there were now three) of my strapping grandsons. Josh, the littlest, was about one year old.

I came home the next day; but I felt uncomfortable from too much sitting, and couldn't wait to stand up and walk about. The feeling didn't go away and I saw a doctor. A locum, I suppose he was; an older man. He listened to my account of the journey, and the pain, and said 'Sounds like haemorrhoids.'

I was surprised. I'm an active person, and I'd never had such a thing, but what did I know? So I got treated for that but the pain came back and one day it dawned on me that the old doctor must have thought I had literally driven the tractor all the way up to North Wales. Four hundred miles on a tractor seat wouldn't just have given me piles, it would've killed me.

Christmas Day itself was non-stop in our household because Adele and Giles, and Hannah and Charmaine, cooked in the restaurant all day long, and we had our own Christmas turkey in the evening. So I thought I'd get Christmas out of the way before I saw to the doctor again. When I saw him in the New Year of 2009 Dr Norris started giving me regular check-ups and blood tests. The blood tests showed nothing. In April, a lady called Dr Patten examined me and referred me to the consultant urologist at West Cornwall Hospital.

He was puzzled and sent me for a biopsy at Treliske Hospital at the beginning of June. I was only 62 and had always expected to be entirely healthy, given the blameless and healthy life I'd lived, so I was a bit impatient with all this.

Then I was sent for an MRI scan. After that I went home and waited for the results. George was working for David Cameron at that time, and he got quite a boost when we knew the Leader of the Opposition was coming to visit Trevaskis. I wouldn't be here though because on the day, Dr Norris rang and said:

'We've got your results but we need further information. You have to go to Plymouth for a CT scan and the consultant can see you today.'

'Oh I can't go today. David Cameron's coming.'

'I'm sorry. This is a hundred times more important. You have to have the CT scan right away.'

So Adele and I drove to Derriford Hospital, Plymouth, where a consultant called Mr Hammond met us. The news was not good. I had a large sarcoma at the base of the pelvis and it would be difficult to remove. Nobody at Derriford had ever performed that particular operation but they were willing to have a go in the next two or three weeks.

So my fortitude was doubly tested. Firstly, there was something badly wrong. Secondly, I couldn't help fearing that the team in Plymouth might inadvertently do further damage in their efforts to put it right. I talked to Serena on the phone that night and the following day she called Mr Hammond. He told her he was glad she'd rung, and said that he would be happy - in fact relieved, was Serena's impression - to have me get a second opinion from a consultant at the Royal Marsden Hospital in London. He referred me to Professor Meirion Thomas, the sarcoma expert there.

I was given an appointment early in August. We went to London and stayed with George and Katy in Fulham. I met Professor Thomas and his fellow surgeon Dirk Strauss. Mr Hammond's diagnosis was right: it was a big sarcoma. I could have the operation in Plymouth or here. I immediately chose to have it at the Royal Marsden because I felt this was the very best place. I'm glad I did make that choice, because at Derriford they'd offered surgery within weeks, whereas Professor

Thomas told me I would need six weeks of radiotherapy before surgery so that the whole area would be as clear of cancer cells as possible.

Adele and I were back in London again in September, for my radiotherapy. We had George and Katy's flat to ourselves because they'd moved to Kew. My farming life at Trevaskis had to continue by proxy. Last year I'd taken some of our British Lops and shown them at Melton Mowbray as a rare breed, and now there was a sale on, but I couldn't take them, so Giles drove them up to Julian Collings, who showed them at the Melton Mowbray sale. The result was amazing. He rang me and said I'd had the top priced boar go for 680 guineas, another at 480 guineas, and an older boar at 250 guineas that went to France.

'You'd better show them every year,' I said.

What a good day. It quite cheered me up.

For six weeks, we spent Monday to Friday in London and weekends at Trevaskis. One time our dear friends from Norfolk came to London for the day. And as the six weeks were ending, I met Dirk Strauss on the stairs at the Royal Marsden and he said

'We've got a date for your operation. Tuesday November 11th.'

We talked about the Armistice Day silence, and I told him I could just about manage a minute, but no longer. In fact I would be out cold for a while, because it was going to be a lengthy procedure. Another Professor, a specialist urologist called Woodhouse, was going to join Dirk and Meirion Thomas.

Adele and I went to see Professor Woodhouse, a good man bringing bad news. He prepared me for what I could look forward to.

'Paul, this surgery will save your life. But it is going to change it forever, too. And I don't want you to be distressed or shocked when you are in recovery so I shall tell you the worst and maybe you can somehow start adjusting to the way you'll have to live.'

Adele took my hand. He went on

'You're going to lose your prostate gland, plus your bladder and most of your lower bowel. What this means for you, Paul, is that you'll have to have two stomas.' He explained what this meant. 'People live with them all the time. They get used to them. And it's the price one pays, unfortunately.'

We talked a bit more. 'You've got a few weeks now before the operation and you need to go home and build up your strength,' he said. 'Do you smoke?'

'I used to, from about fourteen, smoked a pipe. Then when I knew I'd got this sarcoma I stopped.'

'That's good.'

I had learned the hard way that life is real, life is earnest, and to get well I had to help the doctors as best I could.

'What about drinking?' I asked.

'Well, not to excess, obviously,' he said. 'But a pint here and there won't hurt you. If you fancy a drink, have a drink.'

I went home, and worked on the farm. Adele and all the children were all cheerful, helpful and supportive and without their help I would have fallen apart. As it was, I faced up to it.

And there was some good news, before I went back to London: the prospective Conservative candidate for Falmouth and Camborne was to stand down, leaving a vacancy, and George had decided to go for the job. The Boundary Commission had re-drawn the constituency lines, so if the local party selected him, he'd be fighting for Camborne and Redruth. This was not an advantage; there is an industrial heritage in Cornwall and in the past both towns had been strongly Labour.

Just before my operation George thought I needed my mind taking off it so he organised a Wednesday morning visit to the House of Commons to see Prime Minister's Questions. David Cameron came up as we walked along a corridor and said 'Are you going to see PMQ?'

'Well yes,' I said 'But I'm feeling a bit out of my depth.'

'Don't worry about it, that's how I feel all the time,' he laughed. 'I'll give you a wave when it's over.' I sat in the Public Gallery and watched Cameron needling Gordon Brown, the dour Scottish Prime Minister at the time. But when it was all over and he left he did remember to wave. I appreciated that a lot.

I was impressed by the new career George had carved out for himself. 'This wanting to be an MP,' I said. 'What d'you actually want to do, in government?'

'Be Minister of Agriculture, of course,' he said, and grinned.

'Well, that'd be nice.'

For the Sunday night before the operation itself, George had booked us into the Goring Hotel, close to Victoria Station. More impressively, it's about fifty yards from the back gate into the Buckingham Palace garden (42 acres). You can't stay anywhere posher than the Goring. A few years later Kate Middleton would spend the night before her wedding there. And they are famous for their afternoon teas.

We arrived after an arduous journey by train. Typically for a Sunday, we had to put up with engineering work and closures on the line. In the course of changing trains, and platforms, half way, we ran into Julia Goldsworthy, our young Lib Dem MP. We were struggling with our bags and she helped us, which was especially kind of her since we wanted our son to oppose her in the next election, and she knew it.

I slept very well at the Goring. Serena came on Monday morning and she and George ordered a sandwich lunch for all of us; I had to be at the Marsden before two, to have pre-op checks and tests before the rigours to come on Tuesday. Before the pre-op Professor Thomas asked me if I'd received his letter. I hadn't, so he disappeared with the family. He talked seriously to them. He promised that he would do the operation but he wasn't sure what he would find, and there was a slight chance that there might be no useful way to proceed. But he was going to have a good go at this.

I didn't sleep much that first night in Wilson Ward at the Marsden. At eight o'clock the next morning Serena, Adele and George came in. They came as far as the operating theatre at 8.30 before Professor Thomas told them to go and have a coffee somewhere and wait. He would ring them when he had completed the operation.

He called them at 2pm. He'd done it; it was a qualified success and he expected me to recover. There was a slight blip on the heart monitor but the staff were watching it.

I knew none of this, and I wouldn't come round until Wednesday morning, because I'd had several blood transfusions and they wanted me left alone.

So all that was very reassuring for them, and for me, although the reality of recovery was pretty horrible as I had to stay in the Marsden, on Burdett Coutts Ward, because I kept being sick. But the nurses were lovely. And, I had a sweet old gentleman from Twickenham in a bed nearby who told me that next time I came up for the rugby, I could park in his drive.

He unfortunately died about a week later, which shook me badly. And within a few days of that, I was back in the operating theatre, as something had gone slightly wrong the first time and I needed to be opened up again. This time I woke up in excruciating pain in the cardiac care unit, and stayed there for two or three days. I met an interesting Filipino nurse in that unit, always kind, always hard-working, but strangely, he said to me once

'I don't know what my purpose in life is, really.'

Well, if he didn't everybody else certainly did, and I told him so. We could all see he had an outstanding vocation for nursing. He'd worked at the Royal Marsden for 23 years. I couldn't believe he felt so aimless and I said 'You've got an incredibly valuable job here. Everybody you work with looks to you for help when they're stuck – I've seen it. Look how you had to go off this morning and solve a problem.'

I don't think I could have got through those few days without that man. He was a terrific nurse. The Royal Marsden seemed to have the pick of good staff - I never met one who was brusque or unsympathetic.

I was sent back to Burdett Coutts Ward when my heart was steady again, and Adele visited every day and kept me occupied. Because I was so weak I had daily physiotherapy to get me walking again. The physiotherapist was from New Zealand. We had friendly rivalry going on from Day One, because the All Blacks were going to be at Twickenham for the Autumn Internationals on Saturday. Giles would be coming in to see me that morning, because he had tickets for the match.

I told my physiotherapist the All Blacks would be thrashed. She said no, the English wouldn't have a hope. She turned out to be right, unfortunately. On the Sunday, when Adele and George manoeuvred me carefully downstairs, she was the first person I saw and I nearly fell over, but she saved me.

I was in recovery at the Marsden for five weeks; and part of the reason I never got bored was that I got constant updates on the progress of the restaurant, Serena's career and George's big moment. In mid-November George competed against four other contenders to become the Conservative candidate, and won.

The General Election would be in May, 2010. But Julia Goldsworthy, the Lib Dem, had a strong majority.

I was driven home by car from London and it was good to be back again with my dogs and my life around me. But I didn't feel very well, and I felt almost guilty about it, because the whole family came for Christmas of 2009 and it should have been wonderful and I couldn't really be part of it. George brought Katy and her father down. I was up and dressed but I couldn't eat anything at all and all I wanted to do was stay in bed. But I managed to keep going.

I had an appointment to go to London for a check up at 2.30 on Thursday 8th January, and the District Nurse came in often while I was home. I had a bad pain in my pelvis. I struggled to walk more than a few steps and I felt pretty low within myself.

Giles had been going to drive me to the Royal Marsden. The drive takes at least six hours and I didn't think that I would be able to bear it. So we booked a flight from Newquay and a taxi from Gatwick. We got to the airport at 10am for the 11am flight only to find that it was delayed. At last the departure time was set for 1pm. I rang the hospital to explain that we were going to be late and they told us not to worry - they'd see me anyway.

Professor Thomas gave me a thorough check-up and heard about the pain.

'You've got a severe infection in the pelvis,' he said. 'We need to sort that out for you as soon as we can. Can you stay?'

'Well, I'll have to if you want me to.'

'Good - I'll see if I can get a bed.'

He made phone calls and arrangements for them to operate in the morning. I was admitted and Giles caught our flight back from Gatwick on his own. I didn't even have a toothbrush, but the next day Katy went shopping and brought in pyjamas and everything else I needed. While she was doing that, I was under anaesthetic in the operating theatre.

The next morning, I would be prepared for the operating theatre again. Dirk Strauss, the South African surgeon, came to see me on the ward beforehand and described what he had to do. He left with a cheery

'Okay, then. I will see you down there shortly.'

'You'll see me but I won't see you. I've never seen you in theatre yet.' I was expecting to be rolled rapidly into Theatre like a parcel on a conveyor belt but he was at the double doors waiting for me. They were such a great team of doctors and nurses; they did everything they could to make me feel comfortable and in touch with them.

The following week was unimaginably painful. Dirk Strauss had to 'wash out' my pelvis every single day. He told me that when he started the infection was 'up in the nineties'.

That meant nothing to me. 'What should it be?'

'Oh, around six.'

Well, that explained a lot. I gradually got better, and I had Adele with me. She was back in London again and staying in a hotel quite near the hospital. She came into the ward and sat with me, which was very comforting.

I was moved down to the end of the room and I liked it there, close to the bathroom and the airing cupboard. Little things can make such a difference. I could look forward to getting out of bed in the dark and quiet at about 5 o'clock in the morning and having a lovely long hot soak with warm clean towels and clean pyjamas afterwards. One morning I got up and had my usual comforting bath, and was back in bed again when I took a second look at the time. It was only 2am.

In those early months of 2010 there was snow in London, and one day there were no nurses at all because all the buses had stopped and they couldn't get to work. Professor Thomas came in. He said

'We've got a huge backlog, Paul, and we're desperate for beds. Do you have anywhere you could stay in London?'

I told him I could stay with Adele, and I moved into her hotel room for a night. We even met Jane Gould, our friend from Truly Scrumptious, who was in London at the time, and had a meal with her and her daughter and George. But it was icy and I didn't much like the snowy pavements because I wasn't quite firm on my feet.

I was back in hospital when Giles drove up from Cornwall to take us home. I'd been told I mustn't go by train. I was just very pleased to get back to Trevaskis. The dogs made it clear that they'd missed me almost too clear – I had to be careful that Jack didn't push me right over. And then I saw Jilly's new preoccupation. She'd mated with a little dog in December and had given birth to four warm, wriggly puppies. One was going to Giles and Hannah. Their little girl, Scarlett, was one year old now, and a puppy was just what they needed. Another would go to my nephew's mother in law, and we would keep two. We would have four dogs. The cat didn't seem to mind and Jack was happy to be Big Daddy to the pack.

Spring in Cornwall comes early, and I would have loved to get out to the kitchen garden – or even to lay out the new garden around the house – but I couldn't. But I spent time planning what it was going to look like, and thinking how I'd use all the garden-related presents I'd received in the last few months, and which plants I'd buy. I watched Sky Sports. Alan Cook called in at least twice a week. And Adele spent more time at home and less in the kitchens at the restaurant.

Auntie Melba died. My sisters and I had loved her dearly. She and Uncle Johnny Benney had no family of their own. He'd found Prince, my donkey, for me when I was a boy, and when we all went over to Minack to stay, Aunty Melba used to treat us like a little prince and princesses. Such a long time ago, those golden days of childhood.

She'd lived to be 88. I went to her funeral in a new suit. None of my old clothes fitted any more because I was a slightly different shape.

When I eventually decided which plants to buy for the garden, Serena came down to see us and put them in. By April, I was regularly getting visits from the District Nurse and attending the hospital for physiotherapy in my foot and leg. I felt loads better, and organised a get-together of all the men I'd played rugby with when we were young. On our Sponsors' Day, when we sponsored the game against Newquay Hornets, they all came, and so did my cousins who had two sons playing in the Hornets. We had a group photograph taken and I thought how glad I was to be alive.

We were only a month away from the General Election. After thirteen years of Labour Government, ten with Tony Blair and three with Gordon Brown, the polls were predicting now this, now that. I didn't think Labour would win around here and Brown himself was not a popular figure anywhere. It was set to be a close election.

Camborne and Redruth was a new constituency and a three-way marginal seat. The incumbent MP Julia Goldsworthy was still the favourite but her name had been tarnished by some overpayments or careless claims revealed by the expenses scandal the year before. We knew George would have to struggle to defeat Julia, but we also knew that he was well known as a former farmer and grower in the county, articulate and hard-working, and he could win.

In April he entertained Richard Benyon, the Shadow Farming and Fisheries Minister, to a meal in the restaurant, and I was invited. The following day George hosted a Farmers' Breakfast there, and invited all the farmers to meet Richard Benyon as well.

I was knocked sideways by too much socialising, but one thing I knew I could do to help George was get VOTE GEORGE EUSTICE signage erected all over Camborne, Redruth and Hayle. I used to go off in the pickup and trailer with my friend Martin and find well-placed hedges along the roads, then call the farmers whose land it was to check that they didn't mind if we displayed a placard alongside their boundary. It was almost electioneering, because most of them knew me, and by the time we'd agreed the arrangements, I'd made sure they knew who the Conservative candidate was.

It was Martin's job to drive, then park and jump the ditch or scramble up the steep sides of a lane and bash a couple of posts in. When I could, I'd help him to manoevre signs off the flatbed, but I couldn't lift much on my own. I was still too weak.

Election Day was Thursday May 6th; we woke up excited because George had invited us to the count that night, so we'd be there in the Town Hall at Camborne after midnight when the results were announced. We walked in that evening and saw people from all parties milling about, members, activists, friends and relations - everybody glued excitedly to the TV broadcasts. Up and down the country, safe Labour seats seemed to be falling to Conservatives. Even the Liberals had lost a couple already.

By eleven o'clock we knew that our local count seemed to favour George, but it was very tight. A re-count was announced. Julia Goldsworthy was looking strained. Adele, Katy and I were anxious, hardly daring to hope. It was a long few hours. But at about two in the morning the announcement came: George

Eustice, Conservative, 15,969 votes. Julia Goldsworthy, Liberal Democrat, 15,903 votes.

By 66 votes, George had won! Our older son was now George Eustice, MP. We were giddy with delight and pride. He'd worked so hard for this.

We still didn't know whether the Conservatives had actually won the election, but we hoped so. We went home and fell into bed knowing that by morning it would all be clear.

It wasn't, though. To have a majority in the House of Commons one party needed 326 seats. Neither the Conservatives, with 306, nor Labour which had 258, had enough, so in order to get their Bills through the Commons one or another of them had to be able to get a commitment from another party, or (in Labour's case) several other parties. Everybody was watching the Lib Dems, who had 58 seats, to see which way they'd jump.

Nobody knew what was going on and Gordon Brown was still in Number 10.

We set off on a pre-arranged barge holiday at the weekend, along the canals from Bath. Alan Cook had organised it for a small party of friends. It was relaxing, pootling through emerald-green fields past stone lock-keeper's cottages and pubs bedecked with hanging baskets, but unfortunately this was one time when we desperately wanted a TV or a radio. We glided through valleys between wooded hills where there was no reception at all. This, of course, was the whole point of a holiday on a barge, but unfortunately it came at the one time in our lives when we were absolutely desperate to know what was going on in London.

Thanks to the telephone, we did find out that the Lib Dems' talks with the Labour Party had broken down, that Gordon Brown had ordered the removal van for Number 10 and, finally, that the Lib Dems and Conservatives would form a Coalition and David Cameron would be seeing the Queen.

That was Wednesday, and we could now relax. It was a wonderful week, anyway; pure happiness, and good for me although I had to leave most of the lock-gate opening and closing to fitter friends. When I got home I was in excellent form, for somebody who'd had life-changing surgery, and later that summer I helped when Giles took the pigs to shows and sales, and I got to talk to other farmers.

Giles had always liked the pigs. His night club career was in the distant past. He and Hannah had started their own little family; the restaurant was getting more popular with every innovation Giles introduced. George would be making his maiden speech soon. I was much better. Adele was smiling, and May of 2010 was a good time.

Sometimes I look back at the Cornish Bloodbath, and how it has affected us, and I think that even my persecution by Barclays Bank resulted in a few good things. It was an explosion in the quiet agricultural landscape of our lives but it propelled George, Giles and Serena onto new, fulfilling and successful paths.

But what about Adele and me? We were always resilient. We might never have known just how resilient unless we'd lived in a tiny caravan for seven years. I look at the long-term effects, though, and sometimes I wonder.

Since my major operation in 2009 I've had an inguinal hernia, a chronic abscess that has to be drained regularly, half my liver removed, post-operative C-difficile for which I had to be isolated, a fistula – and thanks to Adele and home cooking, plus some exercise, I've managed to regain my appetite and rebuild my body. I weighed only nine stone at one point.

-

In 2012 there was a crisis. I couldn't have another operation but I was in excruciating pain that no amount of morphine could suppress, and Professor Thomas agreed to operate again. I returned to the Burdett Coutts ward, where everybody knew me ('Oh it's him again.') And after the operation, which took four hours, I had a third stoma, which is probably a record. I was in terrific pain, and throwing up all the time, but I was expert at this, now, and Adele was there to support me through the whole horrible experience. I got my appetite back and went home and recovered; and that Olympic summer, along with the unfailing help of Grenville Prouse who'd done wonderful work on my kitchen garden throughout my illnesses, I renewed my interest in organic gardening.

When I was still in London, Adele told me that Alan Cook had bought a boat. To me, in my hospital bed, the idea of idle afternoons in a boat bobbing off a Cornish beach sounded like paradise. Once I was back at Trevaskis I began browsing lists of boats for sale in the *West Briton*. Then one day Giles came in and casually said he'd bought a boat for fishing, off Hayle. He's always been keen on fishing. Nothing lightens the mood like sea air and later that summer I went out on Giles's boat quite often.

A Macmillan nurse visited from time to time. One day I told her I was still quite uncomfortable and she asked how much morphine I was taking. I told her I wasn't taking any. She got that fixed, and by the autumn of 2012, I was pain free for the first time since 2008. I could hardly believe it. I felt years younger, overnight.

Before that, while I was recuperating in bed, I'd got talking to Clive Olds, Adele's brother at St Buryan. He had been on his own since Adele's mother passed away while I was at the Royal Marsden. He needed help to get his farm back on track, and particularly wanted to convert some old farm buildings into cottages. I set about doing a plan. This gave me a lot of creative interest and helped my recovery, I think. I worked with the figures he gave me, and did some calculations. He could move some modern outbuildings to a more suitable spot near the entrance of the farm, and apply for permission to convert the others. I rather enjoyed putting together a plan and it made pretty good sense.

I was strong enough a few months later to talk to him seriously about it. I advised him about his livestock too. I went to see him, we talked, and we remain great friends, but he never has made any changes. I don't think Clive lacks initiative. I just think that a lot of farmers will always think 'if it ain't broke don't fix it.' In spite of everything that went on with Barclays, I think that attitude is as much of a risk as taking on Bezurrel was for me, in 1992.

In pain, you're predisposed to say no to things. Without pain, you can do more than you've ever dreamed possible. I've never felt an urge to climb Everest, but activities you take for granted when you're healthy are major achievements when you're not. Long ago I'd designed and built six farrowing houses at Trevaskis, and Giles asked me if I thought I could make a couple more. My pain was managed now, and I couldn't have been more pleased. I felt I was being useful, and I enjoyed doing it. Enjoyable work is therapy,

I went to the shows again, helping Giles to show pigs at the Devon County and the Royal Cornwall show, and gossiping with all the old South Devon breeders. We even got up north to the Great Yorkshire Show, because our rare breed Lops had qualified to go there. That was unfortunately a total washout, because although the pig show went ahead there were no spectators, one whole day of torrential rain having turned the car park into a quagmire.

Back at home Adele often helped three-year-old Scarlett to bake buns and chocolate cakes. One day Adele took in a small, very weak, piglet, brought her in front of the stove and reared her with milk from a baby's bottle and she thrived. She was just like one of the dogs and would go outside into the garden when the dogs did, and run around, and come back into the house. When somebody knocked and the dogs ran to the door barking, the piglet would run with them. Scarlett used to love picking her up and playing with her. This little creature became a real pet. She remains at Trevaskis to this day, and is called Miss Piggy.

I had tumours on my liver and lungs, which were confirmed by periodic check-ups at the Marsden, but I was loving life; partly because I always have but also because there's nothing like misfortune for making you glad to be alive. I saw old friends, went to rugby matches and tended my garden. George and Katy announced their wedding date: 18th May 2013, in the Chapel at the House of Commons.

By then I'd stayed at a fine selection of London hospitals: the Royal Marsden several times, Sutton, Chelsea and Westminster, the Brompton. In February 2013, I had liver tumours removed and in April, I had a lung seen to. The surgeon had told me that after what I'd gone through already, recovery from the four-hour operation would be 'a walk in the park'. The morning after at 6am I was woken by a phone call from a neighbour at Trevaskis.

'Hallo Paul, Trevor here. Some of your pigs have got out from behind that electric wire you've got. They're over at Lanyon runnin' round the pack-house. You might want to get 'em rounded up before the rest get out – '

'Well I would,' I said, 'except I'm in bed on a ward in the Brompton Hospital in London at the moment, and they took a third of my lung away yesterday.'

There was a silence, then:

'Oh. Oh... I am sorry Paul, I didn't know. I'm sorry I called you. I'll get a hold of Giles.'

I went back to sleep. The surgeon was almost right. The park (Kensington Gardens) was a bit too far for a walk in it, but three days after surgery I was able to walk three times around the Brompton Hospital. It was a late spring that year, but a sudden one. The branches were bare outside the window when I first went onto that ward, but a few days later they all erupted into blossom at once and sparkled against a blue sky.

Serena drove me home after couple of weeks. I wanted to get back for my cousin's funeral. We'd seen too many early deaths. Poor Adrian, my sister's husband, left us in 2009; we'd been close, him and me, towards the end of his life. Charmaine, Adele's beloved sister who had done so much to help build up our business, died suddenly in 2010. Hannah's father died of a brain tumour in 2012. My mother, on the other hand, although she got a little vague before she passed away, lived to be 95 and had a very well-attended funeral at Gwinear Church, with Clare Treloar, aged 80, driving the hearse. And Hugh Lello, my dear friend, lived to a good age.

I have attended so many upsetting funerals in recent years that when I look at the suit I bought new in 2009 I think it's had far too much exposure.

It's hard to believe that any son of mine could arrange his wedding to coincide with the Devon County Show, but that's the younger generation for you. The British Lops got barely a look-in that summer because Giles was going to be George's Best Man and also Head of Catering, up in London. The wedding would be at the Chapel of St Mary Undercroft in the Houses of Parliament, which not many people even see, never mind get married in. As for the reception, the right place was hard to find because there were eighty guests and you couldn't rent a marquee without paying a fortune. Everywhere seemed very expensive. In the end George chose the Inner Temple. We'd decided to do the catering ourselves, which worked brilliantly on the day, although ferrying so much food, drink and hired cutlery - and all the staff - to London, in hired vans, was a bigger operation than we'd foreseen.

We stayed in the Sofitel in St James's and Katy spent her pre-wedding night at the Savoy. One thing we didn't have was buttonholes, so I had to go out first thing on Saturday morning and find some. Fortunately somebody directed me to Liberty's where the entrance off Great Marlborough Street is full of pretty scented flowers, and the florist made some up for me while I waited.

We had Jane Gould with us when we left, in plenty of time, in a taxi from the Sofitel to the House of Commons. Adele and Jane were wearing glamorous hats and high heels and bags and gloves and I was spruced up to the nines with my buttonhole. It's no distance, half a mile as the crow flies, but double that if you set out from the St James's one-way system. There was an NHS demo that day and when our cabbie got to Trafalgar Square and found himself confronted by a shouting procession with banners, he said it would be quicker to walk. Well, quicker if you didn't have to dodge noisy demonstrators and confused tourists and then negotiate admittance to the right part of the House. Of course we arrived late and Adele's feet must have been killing her.

The Chapel of St Mary Undercroft is dazzling; all fan-vaulting and Victorian Gothic, green and red and gold with flickering candles. The ceremony had begun when we slipped into our places at the front. The Reverend Rose Hudson-Wilkin officiated and did a marvellous job. Little Scarlett and Jake were irresistibly solemn in their finery as bridesmaid and pageboy. Natalie my niece has a glorious voice and sang while Katy and

George signed the register afterwards. It was all so exquisitely done, I was quite overwhelmed.

Katy and George were glowing with happiness and I can't remember whether Adele cried but I certainly felt like it. I looked around and saw my cousins, and George's, and many other people from Cornwall besides all the delighted family on Katy's side.

Afterwards we had a family photo-shoot with St Stephen's Tower (Big Ben) in the background, and then we were off to Temple, and some good South Devon roast rib of beef followed by Cornish cream and Cornish strawberries. About the only thing that wasn't from Trevaskis or thereabouts was the wine, but Giles will probably establish a vineyard yet.

We met and talked to a lot of George's political friends, and caught up with family we hadn't seen, and had a wonderful time; and later on, of course, Cornish Pasties came round.

Oh, if John Bloor could have seen us that day.

-

I felt well again. I got a mower I could sit on, which is fun, and began keeping chickens and geese on Trevaskis. I liked poultry when I was a child and it was obvious that visiting children did too. I built an extremely well-appointed house for the geese, and told everybody that they had to have such a smart place to live in because they came from Dartmouth, and that was what they were used to.

Charlie, Serena's son, has grown up to be a top-class rugby player and I went to watch him play at Millfield. The following year he was picked as scrum half for the England Under-16 team. Serena and Nigel had moved up to Cumbria, where his family came from, and were working there. It was much too far from Cornwall, but that summer Serena and I flew out to her house in France. I loved it. A very nice place in a fruit-growing area.

When I got back I was working in the garden when my mobile rang. I straightened up and answered it. George said this was a rushed call, just to let me know that there was a reshuffle and David Cameron had offered him a job.

'Great! What is it?'

'Oh it'll be in agriculture,' he said. 'You'll see. Gotta go to Number 10. He's going to make it official.'

So that was that, and I told Adele who was very excited. We had to wait while he had his interview with the Prime Minister, and then wait some more during some jostling for position with the Lib Dem members of the Coalition, before finding out that George Eustice had been appointed Under-Secretary of State for Farming, Food and the Marine Environment.

Down here at Trevaskis, we went on innovating, figuring out what works. I remembered failing with plums, conventionally planted, in the 80s. We began growing plum trees in polytunnels a couple of years ago and now we've got apples, pleached along posts and wires in the high-yield Spindle system. That was installed around 2014, at about the time when questions were being asked in the House about a certain Acorn Finance, prop, Des Phillips, to which a lot of farmers had lost a lot of money. I'd had a lucky escape.

I felt pretty much as good as new. I pruned fruit trees and helped Giles when he took the pigs to shows. They do win a lot of prizes. We bought a Dorset ram, from Launceston, to breed with our Greyface Dartmoor sheep.

In the summer I thought it was probably time for a check-up and Professor Thomas suggested a scan. So I had one.

And then it was put to me that I might need – of all the things I really didn't want – chemotherapy; but I'd need to see another specialist about that. I was relieved when I did, in a way, because she said I wouldn't have to have it. But not at all relieved about the reason, which was that any kind of intervention now would probably do more harm than good. My insides had been interfered with, with the best of intentions, about as much as they could be.

Charlotte Benson was the specialist.

'The thing is, Paul, yours is a very complicated case, and you're now at high risk if we intervene. You feel healthy, and you look healthy, so I think our best plan is to leave well alone.'

This was welcome news but I was shaken. Fortunately Adele was with me. I had always thought that these doctors were so brilliant that they'd be able to keep me rolling along for evermore. But I had to face facts.

As a distraction after that consultation George gave us coffee in his new grand office at DEFRA. Then we went home and enjoyed the rest of that glorious summer. The weather was warmer than we'd had in years. It was a delight to be outside, with the sun on your back, day after day, and the farm shop and restaurant and farm tours were going great guns. Even my mobility improved, thanks to an expert Chinese masseuse in Truro. Giles and Hannah were going to have a third baby, so we all celebrated.

The only thing wrong recently has been Adele's health. Around the time I had that scan in London, she began to lose weight and feel sick and nobody knew what the matter was. She kept going, as she does, and we decided to go and visit Serena in Cumbria. On our fortieth anniversary I was having radiotherapy, so we didn't celebrate, but we decided to do so on our 43rd. We stayed at Langdale Chase, which we remembered from our honeymoon, and invited Serena and Nigel to a delayed anniversary dinner.

Nearly thirty years ago Adele and Charmaine began spending all Christmas Day making celebration dinners for visitors. They unknowingly founded a whole new hospitality industry in this part of Cornwall, because – especially with so many couples both working – it's since become traditional for a lot of families to come to the restaurant at Trevaskis for the big feast on December 25th and if they can't do that, they'll order their bird from us. At Christmas 2014 we sold and cooked nearly 1,000 birds of different varieties: turkeys, geese, ducks, chicken, guinea fowl, pheasants, partridge...We fill a forty-foot refrigerated lorry every year and employ five full-time butchers, all year round.

Adele began all this with tea and cake for people coming to Pick Your Own.

Joanne Richards stuck by us through the hard times, and we're now among her biggest customers. 'I wouldn't mind betting', she said to me recently 'that one day, you'll get all those farms back.'

I hope to see it. It's summer, 2016 as I write this, and I've just welcomed to Trevaskis eleven new South Devons, descendants of the ones I sold to Julian at Launceston. We live in comfort in our lovely house in the middle of a farm; we have five dogs, two cats, some pigs and a donkey, about forty cows and all the fruit and vegetables growing around us. Apples, cider, hog roasts – we're thriving. Giles and Hannah live in their specially built eco-friendly house just down the lane. George has been re-elected with a bigger majority and he's Minister of State for Farming and Fisheries. And Serena, although separated from Nigel, has three fine sons and the career, as a barrister, that she always wanted. She might not describe it as 'rescuing farmers from vultures' but I certainly would.

We haven't yet regained all the land we lost to Barclays Bank, but that time may yet come. Every life has its troubles but we have risen, fallen and risen again. I do a lot of looking back, because there are times when I'm in pain. But I never give up without a fight.